Y0-AAD-548

TEST MARKETING

CRAIN
BOOKS

Crain Books
740 North Rush Street
Chicago, Illinois 60611

Copyright © 1980 by Crain Communications, Inc.

ISBN: 0-87251-053-0

Library of Congress Catalog Card Number 80-60762

1   2   3   4   5   6

Printed in the United States of America

Contents

2244467

Introduction

To aficionados, it's known simply as Section 2, although some wags initially tagged it Section 8. It first appeared January 1, 1979, as a new center pullout section in *Advertising Age.*

The initial concept still holds. It was developed to provide in-depth coverage of a specific marketing topic—a different topic each week, one not normally covered by *Ad Age,* or covered only minimally. The Section was designed to be pulled out and retained as a ready reference.

And indeed it was.

Reader response was phenomenal. Requests poured in for reprints of specific articles, of entire Sections, to the point where *Advertising Age* was unable to fulfill the requests. Obviously you, the advertising/marketing person, have a hunger for certain information not easily obtainable from other sources. This book, one of a series, is our attempt to meet that need.

This book is not merely a reprint of a specific Section 2. Rather it is a compilation, a gleaning, of all the Section 2 information applicable to the topic at hand. Every effort has been made to ensure that the information included is relevant and up-to-date.

I hope that it will aid you in your work—and more, that you will enjoy reading it.

Kathryn Sederberg
Director, Crain Books

Coping With Recession

BY TOBIE SULLIVAN

NEW YORK—After two years of research and development, Fearless Foods is ready to test new Diamond Dust Donuts—or, rather, almost ready. There's still one more major consideration: The nation's economy is heading into a recession.

The marketing vp, wrought-up about the economic downturn, recommends postponing the project.

The controller counsels cutting out some markets to reduce costs, but the r&d director would rather test fewer variables for a shorter time.

The head of sales predicts that consumers will pass over premium price snacks, while the brand manager insists that they'll shun steaks but still treat the kids to little luxuries—like Diamond Dust Donuts.

The president of Fearless Foods clears his throat. "The economy," he pronounces, "does not dictate our policies—I dictate our policies. Diamond Dust Donuts will roll out in eight cities. Fearless Foods never skimps."

■ Well, hardly ever. Many major manufacturers of package goods consider their businesses and their business procedures "recession proof" or, at least, largely immune to economic factors. Others confess—mostly off the record—to trimming budgets and changing tactics when times are bad.

Although those in the know but outside the corporations are more apt to acknowledge the effects of an economic downturn on the test marketing process, confusion and uncertainty about the economy, about corporate reaction to the economy and about whether to admit to any confusion at all permeates all quarters.

Yet certain trends are appearing through this tangle:

• Decisions about new products depend on the category involved, with hard goods hurting far more than supermarket items or other low price, high volume essentials.

• Few, if any, companies are foregoing test marketing.

• Despite this commitment to testing, companies are consciously trying to save money—a byproduct of the state of the economy—by modifying their approaches. Researchers and execs believe that strategies will place more emphasis on pretesting and include more limited rollouts.

The research director of a major package goods company sums up the situation this way: "To the extent that 1981 will differ from future years, we'd be reluctant to test sensitive categories. Although we haven't dropped anything, we have changed some plans because of economic projections. But we won't give up testing."

Indeed, despite disagreement on the merits of a new product moratorium, professional marketers maintain that the test must go on; any untested entry is barely better than no entry at all.

"We've noticed a decline in food and drug introductions since the fall of 1978," observes Martin Friedman, editor of Dancer Fitzgerald Sample's monthly "New Product News." "But it's hard to correlate figures because of the time lag. It takes one or two years to get test results. To do an average test right, you must reach 3% to 4% of the U.S. population, which can run $250,000 to $500,000, but the investment in new products is a small percentage of a business. If you run across a high-interest product, you'll get it out even in a depression."

■ "We'll do just as much testing as ever—the risks are great in any economy," says Jack Andrews, market research director of General Foods, White Plains, N.Y

Says Al Skolnik, vp-marketing in Revlon's cosmetics division, New York, "We'd move gingerly in a recession, but if there was a definite market opportunity, we'd test." Or, as the advertising director of another "recession proof" company puts it: "You can't run for cover because the sky is falling. Remember, in '73-'74, 5% inflation was considered intolerable. Our aggressiveness is not affected by the economy."

C. Anthony Wainwright, vp-general manager of the Marschalk Co., New York, agrees that such corporate optimism is always appropriate; over-optimism, on the other hand, could be ill-advised. "It's a classic marketing story," he points out. "In a difficult period, marketers who pull back ultimately suffer. If their competitors delayed introductions, it would be okay— but they don't.

"The lifeblood of marketing is conceptualizing, developing and testing. It's a mistake to roll out nationally without reading your markets. A test market is an idyllic controlled situation. Nationally, you have an imperfect situation, distribution problems and fierce competition."

■ Some executives, combining optimism with a knowledgeable assessment of market conditions, go so far as to see opportunity in a downturn. "We'd increase our budgets, because the recession won't last," says Art Williams, president and chief executive officer of Mannington Mills, Salem,

N.J., a manufacturer of sheet vinyl flooring. "We would push the development of new products quicker, but we'd be cautious about pricing and the regions in which we'd test. We wouldn't hold up premium price products, which go to those who don't suffer, and we might spur our efforts on lower price lines. Most of our business comes from remodeling, which increases during a recession. I'd be naive to say we're totally recession proof, but there is that push-pull effect."

A closer look, however, reveals that the economy affects testing in subtler ways. Corporations are reassessing their commitment to standard testing methods and experimenting with less expensive alternatives.

"It costs to make a mistake," says Mr. Andrews of General Foods. "We may be testing fewer products because we do better screening beforehand. We're looking at our money the way the consumer does—we want value and we're cautious."

Those who provide test marketing services have certainly noticed this more budget-conscious trend. "It's more and more difficult to come up with new products," says Arthur Oken, president of Para-Test Marketing, New York, "so companies are getting cautious. They're also becoming more sophisticated, making early predictions based on volume projections and simulations and profit-and-loss models, then making decisions as early as possible."

Adds Larry Karp, vp of Audits & Surveys, New York: "Testing is not curtailed during a downturn. If anything, companies cut back on spending—and go into four rather than six test markets, for example, or make a decision in eight months rather than a year, or test two or three variables rather than four or six."

■ Greg Spagna, president of Market Facts, New York, points out other ways costs are being reduced. "The way we test is the same," he explains, "but the process is more expensive, so clients will save money at other stages prior to testing. They'll use fewer panels with fewer people, or, if they have 18 new product concepts that cost a million dollars each to develop, maybe they'll do four of them rather than eight."

There may be some hazards in these statgies, but research is growing wiser at the same time. "The results [of a lab research test and scaled back rollouts] are still valid," says Mr. Oken, "but it's easier to screw up. I predict there will be more pretesting, more sophisticated analytical programs. Results will be read earlier, and marginal products will be dropped."

Again, though, test marketing ultimately plays the key role. Says the manager of new product development for a major food company that has had nearly 30 years of non-stop profits: "We avoid traps by carefully evaluating expenditures, even though we're probably recession proof because people and pets still eat. Although there are pitfalls when you go other routes, we would use methods other than testing whenever valid. But test markets at least reduce your odds."

If the economy can affect test marketing—albeit in subtle ways—how does it alter consumer purchases of test products? Experts agree that the economy won't prevent the consumer from trying that product—not, that is, if the price is right.

"It depends entirely on the category," maintains Mr. Wainwright of the Marschalk Co. "In difficult times, major purchases suffer first. If you postpone a vacation, for example, you'll compensate by bringing a number of small luxuries into the home. Relatively inexpensive package goods positioned to stretch a meal are idyllic. Some categories did well [in the last economic downturn], and I assume it will be the same now."

"People still buy in a recession," agrees Mr. Oken. "Consumers buy what's put in front of them if they need it and it's positioned properly. As prices go up, though, the consumer recognizes when private labels offer good products."

Others dispute this last point, often frantically. "The consumer does not flock to cheaper products in a recession," protests one exec whose company does not manufacture private label items. "There's real value in branded products." Adds another, "There is some competition with private labels for a certain market—those who buy by price—but there's quality and reassurance in a name brand."

That's what Mr. Andrews and General Foods found in the '73-'74 period. "Our evidence is that when things were really bad the consumer stayed with national brands more," he says. "People switch from chocolate cake to Jell-O, which is still reasonably priced. They get more cautious about impulse buying and want quality assurance. The logic is that when expensive things are out of reach, they'll want better quality in smaller things."

While many manufacturers stress that changes in consumer buying patterns do not affect their recession proof products—and that reductions in sales during the last downturn can be blamed at least partially on nervous retailers who decreased inventories—some admit that test results can be skewed by economic factors.

"We interpreted tests differently [then]," concedes one package goods executive. "We didn't use different techniques—we were just more selective about what categories to test. We were more careful about adjusting and identifying all relevant factors, including the economic environment."

Once again, however, the category counts. "We move rapidly," says Al Skolnik of Revlon. "The cosmetics industry reacts more quickly than package goods."

"The longer you test, the more you're affected by the economy," points out Ann Walsh, vp-marketing of Revlon's cosmetics division. She cites the example of Chaz, brother fragrance to best-selling Charlie, which was tested in drugstores in the last quarter of '78 and rolled out nationally in '79.

"As we did with Chaz, we'd tailor the rollout to replicate the test market," Mr. Skolnik says. "We're more conservative after the introduction. In a close time frame, the economy doesn't matter."

"A recession wouldn't affect our test marketing," Ms. Walsh says. "After all, our plans are based on economic factors."

But market conditions cannot always be built into a test. "Of course external factors influence purchasing and, therefore, test results," observes Mr. Oken of Para-Test Marketing.

"We wouldn't adjust our data much," maintains Mr. Spagna of Market Facts, "but if consumers say they have no money, we'd take it into consideration."

Still, the consumer always finds the funds for certain purchases. "The economy has no major impact on cigaret consumption." says Richard E. Smith, vp-market development for Lorillard. "The only time we've attributed something to the economy was in the early '30s, when tonnage shipped fell back a little. We're recession proof."

Testing—The Ol' Standby

BY JAMES H. BOWMAN

CHICAGO—Scott Wallace recalls what was a new trend in testing new products 16 years ago, when he started in marketing. The idea was to move away from full-scale test marketing, in order to keep your results from the competition, and turn instead to laboratory testing techniques, which would protect your information.

He has no trouble recalling what the trend was in the early 1960s, because they are today's trends also. The more things change in testing new products, the more they remind marketing executives, like Swift & Co.'s Mr. Wallace, of how things used to be.

The word among marketing executives contacted by ADVERTISING AGE is that test marketing is expensive and unwieldy, there are easier and sometimes more accurate ways of deciding when to roll out products and the test itself is never used alone and sometimes not at all. But its usefulness remains, and marketers can't really bring themselves to do without it.

■ "Once we went to the test market to determine if the product would be successful or not. Now we go to confirm our already high expectations based on prior research. At that point, test marketing is a fine-tuning process," said Mr. Wallace, speaking for the Chicago based Swift.

As part of that research, Swift uses a concept measurement technique to determine consumers' readiness to buy and volume estimates techniques to judge what sales might be. Then the company goes to a test market to verify the estimates.

"A lot of money is at stake. Say, a $23,000,000 facility or a $20,000,000 advertising budget," Mr. Wallace said. "You just don't roll the dice with that kind of money on the table unless you are really sure."

Swift also uses the simulated market situation, which has the advantage of secrecy. "Unless the competitor's wife is asked to participate, it's fairly good most of the time, but it still doesn't replace getting into market conditions," Mr. Wallace said.

You can't simulate retailers' or your own sales force's reactions or weather conditions or regional variations, for instance. Testing soup in July is not the same as testing it in January, and you can't get Chicagoans to react like Atlantans.

One common form of testing—one that Swift uses—is the controlled store test. In it, a research company, often units of A. C. Nielsen Co. or Booz, Allen & Hamilton, puts the product into stores in a number of small cities. Such a test helps protect secrecy, because deliveries are made by the research company and not through warehouses, which are ready sources of information for competitors.

Swift, in its deliberations over a product and research approachers, always tests more than one plan, ,Mr. Wallace said, including price, promotion, spending levels and ad campaigns. Then it uses test marketing as "an optimizing procedure."

It used to be a "go or no-go" question that test marketing

5

Soup Starter debuted in test market, but Swiss Miss Lite cocoa mix went directly to national rollout.

answered. Now it's an "insurance policy and optimization process," Mr. Wallace said.

Swift's homemade Soup Starter, for instance, was sold in controlled store tests for six months before being moved to a selling market. By then it was already in a "go" posture, in terms of plant capacity, ordering of raw materials and the like.

■ "We're being a lot tougher about what we bring to market," Mr. Wallace said. The stakes are so high that Swift moves now from test marketing to regional, rather than national, expansion.

Mr. Wallace said he imagines the mortality rate of new products has dropped for marketers in general. "It used to be 50-50 [chance of success]," he said. "Now it's probably up to 80% or 90%. Our mortality rate is zero."

Among other research techniques Swift uses are concept screening, concept quantification and in-home placement. The company also tests advertisement effectiveness and does name re-

search. "Each focuses on a particular aspect, but together they give a sense of where over-all success lies," Mr. Wallace said.

In testing Soup Starter, concept screening "swamped the name research" because it was a "whole new idea" the company was selling, Mr. Wallace said. In identified testing, more than half of the respondents said the soup was as good as their own homemade soup or better—a result the Swift people did not expect.

The testing also showed no discrimination over names. "This doesn't mean the name didn't matter," said Mr. Wallace. "Some very good products have failed because they didn't communicate to the consumer. But on balance more have failed because they were bad products. Good products usually survive bad marketing. And bad ones are led by good marketing to an earlier grave than they otherwise would have had."

■ S. C. Johnson & Son, Racine, Wis., also does upfront laboratory research and traditional marketing research before going into stores, according to Jim Keane, its vp for U.S. consumer products.

"Product evaluation guides" from the research and development staff make placements with consumers, while remaining in touch with r&d chemists. Marketing research personnel conduct traditional larger-scale tests against the competition, such as blind label testing. When the product has "a big name," the researchers do identified paired comparisons in simulated market tests.

Then the company goes either to a controlled store test or to a sell-in situation, where its sales force sells to retailers. In the controlled store test, a new creme rinse, for example, would go into 50 or 60 stores each in South Bend, Erie and Fresno—stores that do at least 80% of the creme rinse business in the area.

The research company staff involved in this test would "put the product directly on the shelves," said Mr. Keane. "The stores have contractual arrangements with the research firms."

Johnson finds controlled store testing ideal when it wants to know more about the product category or is in a hurry to get the product tested. Such testing educates the company before it goes into full testing and gets the product immediately onto the shelves, compared with the six to eight-week distribution for the sell-in approach.

On the other hand, retailers' responses are missing in the controlled store method, because they have agreed ahead of time to stock what the research company brings.

Does Johnson ever go national without test marketing? "I'd prefer not," said Mr. Keane. "But I'm not afraid to if we have a lot of upfront research and if we know the product or idea is a perishable one [that is, others will beat them to it if they delay]. Sometimes you throw the dice, but not out of desperation." Still, the company has never gone through the testing-to-sell-in process without eventually rolling out the product nationally, he said.

■ A recent new product of the Sanna division of Beatrice Foods— Swiss Miss Lite Cocoa Mix—was moved national without test marketing, according to Stephen Wholihan, director of marketing for the Madison, Wis., company.

The product went out in late August and early September after consumer testing on two levels. "There's every indication it will make it," said Mr. Wholihan, though "it's too early to say for sure because we're in the midst of the peak season."

First, there was a taste test to measure intent to buy. In this step, Swiss Miss Lite was pitted against competitor cocoa products. In all, 77% of the respondents—70% of those who don't use low-calorie cocoa products and 84% of those who do—said they would buy the new product.

Then the product was placed in 800 homes, followed by a callback two weeks later. Eighty per cent said they would buy, including an identical 84% who were users and a 76% who weren't.

Sanna looked at these results, especially among lo-cal cocoa users, and at the rapid growth rate in the product's movement before it made what was for the company the unusual decision of going without test marketing. "We thought we could develop a better product," said Mr. Wholihan. "So we did it."

The company has occasionally gone all the way to test marketing and then decided to drop a product, he added.

■ Jovan Inc., Chicago, which sells personal care products, expecially fragrances, does no test marketing. "It takes too long. If we have a good idea, we move fast with it," said Lee Mitchell, director of market research.

Its research consists of shopping mall interviews and (sometimes) checking with retailers. "But to a large extent we trust our own intuition," said Mr. Mitchell, who is not impressed with test marketing in general.

When it comes to its wines—Mogen David Lite, for instance—Mogen David believes in market testing rather than taste testing.

"You hear stories about good test results but poor sales," he said. "Your competitors know what you're trying to do and mess your testing up with promotions and lower prices. A lot of money is spent. Testers go into one little city and hope it is representative."

He said he has a "theory" that managers often use test marketing to cover their mistakes. That's not the case at Jovan, he said, where mistakes are accepted as part of the process.

The wine industry traditionally has not been much for test marketing, according to Bill Keogh, marketing manager of Mogen David, which recently test marketed a table wine—Mogen David Light— sending 12,000 cases to "six or eight" markets. The goal was a certain percentage of the business; and when the company got it, it rolled out the wine nationally.

As far as taste testing goes, Mogen David simply meets its own standards, calling in employes at its Chicago winery at random to see if they like it. "Wine testing is very subjective," said Mr. Keogh. "We don't put a lot of credence in sophisticated testing."

Dancer Fitzgerald Sample
Recommended Test Markets

	Market	Percent of U.S. Households
1.	Albany-Schenectady-Troy, N.Y.	.63
2.	Albuquerque (a).	.36
3.	Amarillo, Tex. (a)	.22
4.	Austin, Tex. (b)	.25
5.	Cedar Rapids-Waterloo, Ia.	.38
6.	Chattanooga, Tenn.	.33
7.	Cleveland.	1.75
8.	Colorado Springs-Pueblo	.25
9.	Columbia-Jefferson City, Mo.	.18
10.	Davenport-Rock Island-Moline, Ia.-Ill. (b)	.41
11.	Des Moines	.45
12.	Duluth-Superior, Minn.-Wis. (a).	.22
13.	Fargo, N.D.	.26
14.	Grand Rapids-Kalamazoo-Battle Creek, Mich.	.66
15.	Greenville-New Bern-Washington, N.C. (a)	.30
16.	Greenville-Spartanburg-Asheville, S.C.-N.C. (a).	.68
17.	Indianapolis	1.03
18.	Jackson, Miss.	.34
19.	Jacksonville, Fla.	.45
20.	Kansas City, Mo.	.86
21.	Knoxville (b).	.49
22.	Lexington, Ky. (a)	.29
23.	Louisville	.58
24.	Memphis (b).	.72
25.	Milwaukee (b)	.92
26.	Mobile-Pensacola, Ala.-Fla. (b).	.45
27.	Nashville (a).	.79
28.	New Orleans (a)	.69
29.	Norfolk-Portsmouth-Newport News-Hampton, Va.	.58
30.	Oklahoma City (a)	.64
31.	Orlando-Daytona Beach (b)	.63
32.	Paducah-Cape Girardeau-Harrisburg, Ky.-Mo. (a)	.36
33.	Peoria, Ill. (b).	.28
34.	Portland, Ore.	.92
35.	Richmond, Va.	.51
36.	Rochester, N.Y.	.43
37.	Rockford, Ill.	.23
38.	St. Louis (b).	1.31
39.	San Antonio (a).	.58
40.	Savannah, Ga.	.17
41.	South Bend-Elkhart, Ind.	.37
42.	Springfield-Decatur-Champaign, Ill. (b).	.38
43.	Tampa-St. Petersburg (b)	1.18
44.	Tucson.	.27
45.	Tulsa (a)	.52
46.	Wichita-Hutchinson, Kan.	.52

Notes: 1. Markets with below average income are marked (a). Those with above average income are marked (b).
2. Markets with a high proportion of Spanish speaking population are Colorado Springs-Pueblo, New Orleans and San Antonio.
3. Markets that should be used with caution because they have been "over-tested" are Kansas City, Milwaukee and Portland.
4. Tampa-St. Petersburg has a disproportionately high population of the 50-plus age group.

Source: Dancer Fitzgerald Sample, "A Guide to Test Market Media Planning and Market Selection," fourth edition, January, 1979. The list is under review and will be updated shortly.

Sharpening Market Tests

BY TOM WATTS

CHICAGO—"Unprecedented anxiety," in the words of one top agency research executive, is what's prevailing in test marketing these days. And it's influencing a growing tendency by researchers to expand preflight tryouts of new products to new geographic areas coast to coast.

It isn't that Fort Wayne, Ind., for years the nation's top test market, is being abandoned. It probably still heads the list of guinea pig cities, but there's a continuing trend to use more than one market at a time to get a broader and—theoretically—more accurate guess on whether a product will sell, for how much and at what cost-effectiveness per media dollar.

The pulse-taking practitioners seemingly haven't come up with radically new testing processes, but they're putting some new wrinkles on the old standbys.

■ An ADVERTISING AGE survey indicates that test marketing specialists are under increasing pressure by agencies and clients in their efforts to sharpen their predictions—or educated guesses.

That's partly because market tests, like everything else, are more costly than ever, and so is the financial risk of launching a new consumer product.

Fort Wayne, of course, has long been regarded as "America in microcosm" because it just about matches the national norms demographically and economically. And it has the added advantage

of being relatively isolated from "foreign" media. The city's two newspapers and three tv stations provide what are considered excellent litmus paper tests to judge the effectiveness of ad campaigns for fledgling products. Fort Wayne's 25 shopping centers may stock as many as 15 test products on any given day.

But the researchers continue to reach out, particularly toward the Sunbelt markets, "where the people are going," says David Berger, senior vp-research director of Foote, Cone & Belding, Chicago.

"Researchers are giving up the idea that any one town reflects the country," Mr. Berger says, "and they're seeking more and more medium and medium-small towns in their efforts to test a new product's appeal in more than one place at one time—and keep costs down."

■ An exception: Mr. Berger's own agency tested Sunkist orange soda in, of all unlikely and atypical places, New York City. "Very successfully, too," he says, "but whether that proves or demolishes the general rule, I don't know."

More typical test towns now widely used include Phoenix, Dallas, Tucson and Little Rock. Other intensively used markets for testing products, pitches, pricing and profitability are Fresno; Memphis; Des Moines; Omaha; Grand Rapids, Mich.; Kansas City, Mo.; Spokane, Wash.; Indianapolis; Davenport, Ia., and Denver.

Vern Churchill of Chicago's Market Facts, a major company in the test marketing field, says his orga-

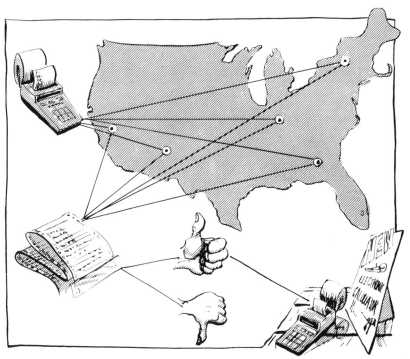

From conception to test market towns to data analysis, that thumbs up sign remains elusive for the new product in its quest to reach the market shelves. A thumbs down, of course, means it's back to the drawing boards.

nization has permanent test staffs in Erie, Pa.; Syracuse and Binghamton, N.Y.; Wichita; Fresno; Spokane, and Little Rock, as well as in Fort Wayne. These cities, he says, "were selected by the same old criteria we've used in the past—demographics, economic climate, purchasing power, trade acceptance. We use cities large enough to provide valid samples but not so large that they cease to be cost-efficient."

■ Market Facts uses controlled store testing, as it has for 13 years, in its eight selected cities, distributing, auditing sales and stocking shelves on a fee arrangement with cooperating stores.

A. C. Nielsen Co., another major test marketing company, is using Tucson; Boise, Ida.; Peoria, Ill.; Green Bay, Wis.; Savannah, Ga., and Portland, Me., to test new products.

Ad-Tel, a member of the marketing services group of Booz, Allen & Hamilton, is zeroing in on Charleston, W. Va.; Bakersfield, Cal., and the Quad Cities of Davenport and Bettendorf, Ia., and Moline and Rock Island, Ill., as prime product test markets. Again, the self-contained nature of these markets is an important consideration in their selection.

But back to that anxiety some research practitioners seem to feel: People such as Mr. Churchill of Market Facts dismiss the prevalent suspicion about the accuracy of long-established test areas.

He believes consumers in even much-researched markets such as Fort Wayne have yet to become consciously aware that they are testing tomorrow's products today (though only about 45% of products tested ever reach nationwide mass distribution).

■ Mr. Churchill says controlled test stores appear perfectly normal to shoppers. Consumers, he says, buy what's on the shelves—though theoretically they'll buy more of a given product if it is backed by an effective ad campaign in local media.

One advantage of simultaneous multiple-market testing appears to be the opportunity to test more than one creative concept for a particular product. Agency creative departments, understandably, tend to take a dim view of this practice, but client pressure—that old search for an absolute yardstick showing product acceptance per advertising expenditure—is making such combined product-and-pitch testing more prevalent.

Though many major agencies do get deeply involved in test marketing and site selection, William Wells of Needham, Harper & Steers, Chicago, for one, prefers to leave new product testing mechanics to the specialist companies such as Ad-Tel, Market Facts, Marketing Research Corp. of America, Audits & Surveys and McCallum & Stielman in Manhattan. But he certainly does get involved in the media selection and the campaigns that support test marketing.

■ There's little new in marketers' endless search for some magic formula that can pinpoint what amount of advertising has how much influence on sales. As retailer John Wanamaker is said to have lamented: "I know that half the money I spend on advertising is wasted. The trouble is, I don't know which half."

That's true of every product marketed to this day, says the chief of a market research company. And the nagging questions multiply in the case of introducing new products. Wasteful or not, the ad campaign backing the newcomer may and usually does have enough impact to create some degree of brand awareness and even a willingness to try it. Once.

But compounding the problem for test market researchers are other little questions, such as whether there's really a market for a new product, whether people will buy it more than once, whether the packaging is right and how it will stack up against competition.

There is, the experts agree, no crystal ball that works.

But the hunt for one never stops for the obvious reason that billions of dollars are involved in new product introduction and millions in testing their potential.

What makes clients nervous is that payroll, shipping, capital projects and the like routinely go through cost-benefit studies that are near absolute. Most ad budgets aren't subjected to that sort of review and couldn't stand it.

■ Nabisco researchers think they might be on the right track after years of exhaustive tests of products and the ads designed to move them. *Dun's Review* (September, 1978) reports that Nabisco has stuffed a computer with some 2,000,000 scraps of data in the hope that they'll be able to pinpoint the ideal amount of advertising required per product and also calculate the most profitable way to allocate ad dollars among products.

Less computer-conscious admen figure that, given five years of experience with a product and its advertising rationale, you can make a fairly shrewd judgment. Procter & Gamble tested Pringles potato chips for three years in Evansville before going national, but that's hardly typical, even for other major companies such as General Foods, Ralston Purina, General Mills, Green Giant and Kraft Foods.

For advertisers and agencies not blessed with that kind of money and that much time, finding a fail-safe test indicator is even more frustrating.

In captive store testing, there's the problem of higher fees demanded by store chains, based on sharply higher marketing costs. Perhaps as a result, researchers seem to be putting added stress on, and confidence in, small sample "lab tests."

There are five or more specialist companies in this facet of test marketing. In such tests consumers typically are given the new product to try, then quizzed on their attitudes toward it. Ad campaign tests often are included as part of the product tests.

■ Says one agency true believer in the lab method: "You use maybe 400 people and spend $30,000 to $50,000 instead of maybe $1,000,000, and you can wrap things up in 10 weeks, as opposed to 10 months to a year in conventional test marketing."

He admits there is a defect to be considered in lab testing: "Lab testing gives you a better product trial acceptance than it does a reliable indication of repeated buying intention. In that sense, it may be a bit artificial. And a projection of repeat sales is the greatest need and the hardest to get."

So—the probing and the pondering—and the anxiety—continue.

"There ain't no **Rosetta Stone** in this racket," says one harried tester.

What Are the Alternatives?

BY JENNIFER ALTER

CHICAGO—As the new decade brings fast-paced shifts in demographics and great technological innovation, companies are facing the need to reevaluate the entire concept of test marketing.

One element sure to affect the status of test marketing in the '80s is the evolution of simulated or laboratory testing.

With this process, consumers are introduced to a product, normally with advertising, at a shopping center. They purchase the product and researchers chart their reactions, providing regular measurement of buying behavior. This method of testing, in one form or another, has been in use for a number of years and is growing more sophisticated all the time. Opinions vary on the over-all effectiveness and ultimate potential of the simulated system—be it Management Decision's ASSESSOR, Eldridge & Lavidge's COMP or Yankelovich, Skelly & White's Laboratory Test Market—but most manufacturers contacted by ADVERTISING AGE agree that it is a useful addition to the marketing process.

At the same time, company execs agree: As a screening technique, simulated testing is valuable, but there is no substitute for a real test market.

One company high on the merits of the laboratory test is General Mills, Minn. "We use it quite routinely and have been for several years," says John Newman, marketing research director of the Bet-. ty Crocker division. "The primary function is to screen project candidates for test, as test marketing is extremely expensive. It's hard to do for under $750,000, it's time consuming and it's revealing to the competition."

Premarket volumetric testing, as Mr. Newman calls it, "eliminates the dogs and also gives you a better sense of what to expect and what to look for, and it helps you establish support levels." One of the few contacted who said he conceivably would go national with a product after very strong results from a pretest, Mr. Newman is still committed to the real test under most circumstances.

"Even if you're quite confident the volume is there, there are other reasons for test marketing," he says. "It provides a shakedown on a miniscale and an opportunity to check out marketing plans.

Mr. Newman, who says he relies mainly on National Purchase Diary's Estimated Sales Potential (ESP) and Market Audit's BASES, believes that the simulated test will become more prevalent. "Because of the huge scale of test market tests, it is inefficient to try too many alternatives," he says. "But premarket volumetric tests lend themselves to experiment. You can test different names, prices, packages and quantities. There are a lot of options and decisions and pretesting helps you select the most attractive offer to test market."

A less enthusiastic advocate of laboratory testing is Charles Hildreth, associate director of client services in the development de-

How test marketing stacks up

The following tables, compiled by Market Facts, are based on questionnaires sent to the market research directors of the 132 largest consumer goods manufacturers in the U.S. A total of 84 were returned—a 64% response rate. The responses were obtained from March 30 through April 20 in 1979.

Use of Test Marketing Techniques

	Regular test markets with outside auditing %	Controlled store testing %	Test marketing laboratories %	Test market purchase diaries %	Test market telephone tracking studies %
Usually use it in conjunction with other research techniques............	92%	86%	84%	95%	100%
Usually use it autonomously.................	8	14	16	5	—
Average number of times used in past year.........	3.6	3.2	3.4	3.3	3.7

Source: Market Facts.

Importance of Test Marketing Techniques

PERCENT OF RESPONDENTS WHO SAID:

	They spent most money on last year	Technique growing in use	Declining in use	Net difference
Company managed test markets, with outside contract auditing.............	12%	10%	12%	− 2%
Controlled store testing (i.e., Marketest, Market Audits, Nielsen Data Markets..........	10	11	7	+ 4
Test market laboratories (i.e., Yankelovich, ASSESSOR, COMPAC)........	8	16	4	+12
Test market purchase diaries......	4	6	6	—
Test market telephone tracking studies......................	7	12	5	+ 7

Source: Market Facts.

Test Marketing Usage

		Product Line		Research Budget	
Used in last year:	Total sample	Grocery & drug products	Durable goods & services	Under $1,000,000	Over $1,000,000
Company managed test markets...............	38%	58%	20%	22%	70%
Controlled store testing.....................	32	51	12	26	44
Test marketing laboratories.................	27	42	12	18	44
Test market purchase diaries...................	28	46	10	11	63
Test market telephone tracking studies.............	48	74	20	3	82

Source: Market Facts.

Technique Receiving Most Spending

	1979 survey	1978 survey	Net change
Company managed test markets, with outside contract auditing..	12%	15%	− 3%
Controlled store testing (i.e., Marketest, Market Audits, Nielsen Data Markets)..	10	19	− 9
Test market laboratories (i.e., Yankelovich, ASSESSOR, COMPAC).............................	8	10	− 2
Test market purchase diaries..	4	4	—
Test market telephone tracking studies............................	7	11	− 4

Source: Market Facts.

partment of General Foods, White Plains, N.Y.

"Their accuracy has been over-claimed," Mr. Hildreth says. "We would never go straight out [nationally] on their results."

In fact, Mr. Hildreth indicates that GF does not use simulated testing methods particularly often and has not used them at all in the past year or so.

He cites some dangers in relying on simulated programs. "We are concerned that on first blush (the product) may be good but that long term it drops." And he adds, "There is a tendency to want to believe in the results in terms of share performance, and this can be misleading."

GF would use simulated tests, Mr. Hildreth says, for diagnostic purposes. "These tests help you understand what you have done and how to improve, what's good about a product, what makes it work," he says.

Swift & Co., Chicago, according to Bruce Gooden, director of new products, sees clear advantages to simulated testing.

"If our ability to produce the product is very expensive, we make a small amount and test the water to decide, yes, we should spend $250,000 to put the machine in," he says. "We might also use it where the proposition has been very gray; the product is not a clear winner or loser, and you don't feel real good about taking a market loss because of the questionable success."

Another instance in which Mr. Gooden sees simulated tests as effective is when the product needs its total package—all consumer communications—in order to sell. "Merely telling someone about it isn't going to do the trick. There has to be something more personal about it," he says. "And the lab allows you to expose people to your package itself in a competitive framework.

Mr. Gooden also cites the advantages of confidentiality afforded by the simulated test, and considers it one of the few methods of test pricing. He says it provides a clearer diagnosis of the situation than does test marketing in that you're able to separate which results come from coupons and which come from advertising.

Lastly, Mr. Gooden says, because of its expediency, a lab test is useful for a seasonal product. The ability to move quickly enables the manufacturer to get the product right out rather than wait around for another year.

■ Mr. Gooden points out that Swift has never foregone a test market after a lab test. After all, he says, a lab test won't tell you what level of distribution to aim for, what shelf space you will get, whether you will be featured in trade ads, what your competition will do, what kind of repeat sales you will have and what true level of sales the product will reach.

Mr. Gooden, who has used Management Decision's ASSESSOR, says he applies the method only if the company is insecure about a product. The company, he says, has gone ahead with only one of four products it has screened in a lab situation.

■ Perhaps the general feelings toward laboratory testing are best summed up by Joel Levine, corporate director of research for Pillsbury, which uses its own "Supertest" system. Mr. Levine says Pillsbury kills about one of three products after the Supertest and would never consider going national without a test market.

"There are too many risks," he says. "Even if you get a pretest volume that is great, how big is it really? We use the Supertest to get some feel, some perspective on how good the market is. The objective is to be more selective with what you take into test."

Hershey's Whatchamacallit candy: Chicago and Detroit

Schweppes U.S.A. mineral water: West Coast

Procter & Gamble Coldsnap dessert: Dallas and Denver

Pillsbury Microwave Hungry Jack pancakes and popcorn: Chicago. Milwaukee and Minneapolis/St. Paul

Nestle Co. "Brownie" and "Blondie" mixes: Indianapolis and Milwaukee

Kraft Good Guys snacks: Cincinnati

These products were test marketed. Would laboratory testing have helped?

Laboratory Testing— The Background

BY ROBERT GOLDBERG

NEW YORK—A war ended in 1945 and another began.

The second war—which, 30 years later, is still increasing in intensity—is a battle for the heart and dollars of the affluent American consumer.

Before the returning GIs streamed off the troopships in '45, new products as we know them now simply did not exist. Nor did the need to refine the process of introducing new products into the marketplace.

Far-reaching changes that would reshape the market climate for consumer goods, particularly package goods, were to take place.

The New Age Dawns

The new home-owning suburbanites had to be fed and clothed. With investment capital available, retailers formed *chains* of supermarkets. The retailing revolution brought with it a more scientific outlook, centralized buying policies and greater central control over product support policies at the store level.

The specialty merchants, with their "mom and pop" stores and their emphasis on personalized service, declined as outlets for package goods.

Robert Goldberg is Senior VP-Director of the Yankelovich, Skelly & White Co., Laboratory Test Market Division in New York.

The retailing revolution and the new monolith, television, were changing the landscape of American marketing forever.

Leading marketers—instinctively, accidentally or by careful reasoning—saw that the newly affluent consumer demanded new products, prompting a shift in marketing philosophy.

Altered was the historic belief that a new product could be added to a salesman's existing line and made profitable by using sales incentives—either performance rewards or threats of unspecified punitive action.

With the arrival of tv, this nearly total dependence on manipulation of the sales force was replaced by the "marketing approach."

Elements of the "marketing approach" included the following conditions:

● Brands could be successfully introduced—even if only marginally different from existing brands—if consumer advertising could generate sufficient demand. The rule that a new product had to represent a true breakthrough was relaxed.

● New product marketing plans were developed and used. They included statements about target markets (in those days the entire household), advertising strategy that included themes and media and promotion strategies, such as sampling and couponing.

● Formal business plans that provided management with a basis for determining a new product's sales and profit performance were prepared.

The business plan included estimates of potential market share or dollar volume, estimates of recommended spending levels and a timetable for the breakeven point and the start of profit delivery.

Risky and Expensive

Compared with today's sophisticated marketing plans, the earlier variety might appear primitive. But they achieved the goal of changing the emphasis to consumer "pull-through" from sales force "push-through."

The very act of forming marketing plans with crucial target "numbers" was an indication that the dollar risk of new product introductions was increasing rapidly. Increased risk meant more new product failures at more expense. The need for risk-reducing techniques was clear, and the conventional test market appeared to be the answer.

By limiting and containing product introductions, the test market provided answers to several key questions: Was the projected potential sales volume on target? What advertising and promotional levels were required? Did the projected profitability timetable seem reasonable?

The advantages of the test market concept seemed clear. Yet there were skeptics.

Some marketers wondered whether cities such as Fort Wayne, Peoria, Des Moines or Rochester—independently or together—could provide feedback allowing marketers to predict a new product's performance accurately on a national level. Also, the "my wife loves it so why waste time test marketing it" approach was very evident.

As more and more new products went the way of the Edsel, however, resistance melted and disappeared.

Now, more than 20 years since the conventional test market became a way of life for marketers big

and small, the climate again has changed.

The test market may have its limits.

With the sands of consumer demand continually shifting, the effectiveness of new product introductions can make or break a company. The industry is less tolerant of failure, as are boards of directors, stockholders and investment analysts whose expectations are based—perhaps unrealistically—on the success performances of another era.

What are these changes, which once again have altered the face of marketing? They include the following:

• A leading brand in a given market segment can enjoy no more than a 5% to 10% market share. And in some categories a winner may be 1%.

• All but the giant marketers have difficulty obtaining distribution and effective shelf space.

• Post World War II optimism has dissipated, as has the excitement of acquiring possessions.

• Interest in intangibles, services, self-realization and personal recognition has grown.

• The birthrate has dropped.

• Consumer interest in personalized brands has been battling with an equal interest in simplifying life.

• Major marketers have recognized the importance of new products to their growth.

In short, market conditions are tougher, hurdles are higher and the size of the possible rewards for each individual product are smaller.

And the concept of the conventional multicity test market, meanwhile, has come under fire. Why? Using the conventional technique, feedback now appears to be less conclusive.

In the past, if the target market share for a new product was 35%, for example, a larger margin for error was allowed. Now, such a margin can be fatal—and expensive.

The conventional test market is ever more vulnerable to actions by competitors.

With the advent and primacy of tv as an advertising vehicle, moreover, expenses have skyrocketed.

Increased pressure on marketers to reduce new product introductory timetables conflicts with the parameters of conventional test markets.

Diagnostic data on the success or failure of a product in test market are increasingly difficult to gather.

A Laboratory Solution?

It appears that the market conditions of the 1970s and the imperfect fit of classical test marketing to these new conditions call for new tools or for modifications of the familiar ones.

One not-so-new tool, simulation, overcomes many difficulties now inherent in "real world" tests. Because both time and space are compressed in the test process, the simulation/laboratory approach allows each element of a real world test to act upon a consumer.

It provides a mechanism for generating product awareness and a means of tapping into trial interest, if that interest is genuinely present.

The laboratory test gives the consumer an opportunity to "buy" and to "invest" while giving a marketer the chance to collect vivid immediate feedback on consumer decisions. It also provides a mechanism for finding out how and how often a new product is used in the home and what products—if any—it displaces.

So far, the successful prediction ratio of laboratory test markets has been at least as high as the multicity tests. The lab tests have been performed, moreover, in far less time and for much less cost.

But despite all this, they can still be improved. New directions being taken by the laboratory technique include categories other than packaged goods, softwear items, appliances and even certain services, for example.

In the end, however, it remains to be seen whether the laboratory technique will ultimately supplant the classical test market.

But as the marketing war reaches its apex, it appears that the laboratory test market achieves the goals of any good commander: It helps win the battle and keeps casualties to a minimum.

Laboratory Testing — What's Available?

BY JAN ZWIREN
AND VINCE COPP

CHICAGO—It's sitting on your desk, still with the code number assigned to it. Everyone thinks it's a great idea. Especially you. (It was your idea to begin with, no matter what anyone in r&d says! Right!)

Your boss is skeptical, but budgets are approved because the preliminary financial analysis shows a break-even point in 24 months on a cumulative basis from the start of the project. It also meets the return on investment criteria established by your company.

But that's all on paper. And it's only as correct as the assumptions you, your agency, the financial planning people and who ever else is involved in the process have made.

■ Here's an eye chart that might help you see things a little more clearly:

```
SPRINTER SPECS

MAP TELE-RESEARCH

ADTEL TRIM

ASSESSOR COMP LTM
```

Jan Zwiren was vp-marketing at Helene Curtis Industries until she left to establish her own ad agency. Vince Copp, who was director of marketing research at Helene Curtis, has joined the Jan Zwiren Agency as vp-marketing and research.

It's not really an eye chart. It's what today's marketer has at her or his fingertips when she or he seeks help in evaluating new products before test marketing. Helene Curtis Industries is familiar with most of them, has used many on the list and can verify the validity of those used. Luckily, some of the successes are on the retail shelves and, luckily, some misfires went no further than laboratory testing.

We are not going to recommend a particular service or method, and certainly the list does not include everyone. But it should provide a basic understanding of the major sources available and how they can help in one of your most critical areas of responsibility—new products.

In deciding which method to use, you must first define what you need from such a system.

■ If you are primarily interested in screening new products after initial concept and new product testing has been done, then you may want to use a new product screening model such as SPRINTER (Management Decisions Inc.).

Advertising agencies might also have mathematical new product models, SPECS (the N W Ayer Advanced Methods Group), for example.

These systems are strictly mathematical models that perform a computer simulation of the likely behavior of a new product in the marketplace. Naturally, such systems are heavily dependent on the assumptions fed into them.

Once you have a product and your agency has developed advertising for it, you may want to measure how much consumers are motivated to try the product after being exposed to the commercial. Methods such as MAP (McCollum/Spielman) and Tele-Research provide such readings via pre/post-brand switching, coupon redemption rates, etc.

These systems also include facilities for contacting respondents after they have had a chance to use the product in their homes. Measurements can be obtained on product satisfaction, usage patterns, repeat purchase intent and shifts in attitude after the initial exposure to the commercial.

While these methods do not provide market share projections, they do offer benchmark data that allow you to judge the viability of your product/concept both in absolute terms and against alternative positionings.

Once you have selected a final product formulation, package, pricing structure, name, commercial and other elements of the marketing mix, you may want to measure how they work together before risking the dollars and full competitive knowledge of a formal test market. You basically have two choices: A mini/micro market approach or a comprehensive laboratory system.

The mini/micro market approach uses actual stores adding to the reality of the test. Moreover, it can expose the product to competition on a limited basis.

The ADTEL mini-market approach uses a dual-cable CATV system, controlled store distribution and purchase diary panels to provide market share measurement similar to a formal test market and in about the same time, six months.

The Trim micro-market approach uses state-of-the-art optical scanning equipment at checkout counters to measure the Universal Products Code of the test product and competitive products in selected food chains. Sales movement

and share can be read weekly but can't be projected nationally because of the relatively small samples of stores and only one type of outlet for measurement.

▪ If you want a projection of your market share or a test of different variables in the marketing mix, based on alternative levels of advertising expenditures, awareness, distribution, etc., in about 12 weeks, you should consider a comprehensive laboratory model such as LTM (Yankelovich), COMP (Elrick & Lavidge) or ASSESSOR (Management Decisions). While there are a number of major differences in the three, they are similar in their basic approaches of:

• Exposing qualified respondents to a commercial within an environment of competitive ads.

• Allowing consumers to purchase the product in a simulated store environment to obtain a trial measurement.

• Recontacting consumers to measure satisfaction and repeat purchase intention.

• Providing diagnostics on advertising and product positioning.

The micro and comprehensive lab approaches take time and money. Their use is as much an art as it is a science. Don't use them if you're not prepared to wait for the final results or act upon the findings.

Meanwhile, there are a number of key points to keep in mind before undertaking a simulation:

1. Simulation cannot be expected to be a panacea for all new product woes. While these methods can help improve batting averages by providing diagnostic information that can help direct improvements in product formulation, positioning or advertising, these systems cannot be expected to substitute for creativity in product work.

2. Simulation must be made an integral part of your current new product evaluation system. Summarily adding it to the new product repertoire is about as ineffective as haphazardly putting out a line extension merely to increase net sales short term.

The key concept here is preplanning. Laboratory suppliers should be brought into the picture at the beginning of the new product evaluation process. Most of these people are very knowledgeable and can help select factors and design diagnostic questions that should be asked during both the early concept tests and later in the laboratory simulation.

By relating all the various pieces of the new product evaluation process at the onset, a self-validating or, at worst, an invalidating system will be created.

3. Laboratory simulation is *not* a substitute for current parts of the new product evaluation system, such as pretesting of commercials, even though laboratory simulation covers many of the same areas. Not only would it be an expensive way to do advertising or product testing per se, but it would affect the real purpose of simulation: To test the interaction and synergism that takes place when all the individual pieces of the marketing mix are put together.

4. Selection of the specific simulation system depends on the specific nature of the new product venture.

For example, with a potentially hot new brand that may be highly vulnerable to competitive preemption, it might be wiser to use a comprehensive lab test market. This is especially true if plans are made to invest heavily in advertising and sampling in order to drive the brand share up to a relatively high level. In this situation, an extremely accurate projection of brand share would be desirable. Besides the reassurance such a projection would bring, it just might provide the criterion for deciding whether to go immediately to a national launch without going to formal test market.

On the other hand, a micromarket test in the marketplace would be preferred if interest were in an alternative sampling program for a new product launch or

in the measurement of the incremental gain of a line extension.

This would be especially true in the case of line extensions where comprehensive lab systems have difficulty making accurate projections of low brand shares (*i.e.*, if I'm one share off at the 10% share level, I've only made a 10% error, but if I'm one share off at the 2% share level, I've jumped to a 50% rate and 100% at the 1% share level.). In this situation, the micromarket's ability to read directional viability is more important.

5. Even though we have used and highly recommend lab testing, it has a few other limitations.

The most serious is that the *product must fit into an existing product category*. If you have been extremely creative and are prepared to open up a new category, congratulations. Be equally creative now and be able to devise your own method of testing its market potential, since laboratory testing systems will have no norms on new categories.

If any *major new competitive* brand were put into test market or launched nationally in the category you're entering without being included in the laboratory test market, the results may be grossly overstated.

In addition, lab test marketing methodology does not really take into account the various types of competitive reactions that may take place in entering a category (such as dropping millions of coupons, increasing ad weight, reformulating and all those other fun things competitors do to give you a headache). A larger competitor may quickly match your preemptive positioning and significantly outspend you in the process, gaining far greater awareness for the product positioned against you.

Most important, *the accuracy of the market share projection is heavily dependent on your own assumptions* on such key marketing variables as levels of awareness, facings achieved and distribution.

Be honest; put in levels you believe your company can attain.

Look at historical data to help the accuracy of projections.

Also, think of the human element in marketing. If the sales force has been against the product from the onset, don't look for 85% distribution during the introduction period unless the product is being backed by a significant campaign and promotion dollars neither they nor the trade can refuse.

■ All of these problems now noted, there are still other considerations in the testing process. For one, even before a laboratory test marketing project is begun, answers should be anticipated. Preparing a matrix of possible results and reactions is handy.

If results put you in the black, for instance, pat yourself on the back. You have a probable winner. But you will now have to quantify how big a winner.

Have marketing plans prepared for formal test markets to ascertain how high is up. The test could measure various advertising weights or vehicles, sampling and promotional programs. If results go national, plan to use several markets for fine-tuning ad weights and promotions.

If, on the other hand, results are red, don't fire the new products directors, marketing research director or agency hastily. They've done their jobs in preventing a bomb and they're just as disappointed as you.

If, as is most often the case, results fall into the infamous gray area, don't just stand there biting your nails, hitting your head on your desk muttering, "Why me!"

This could be a time to exercise some real creativity.

■ Don't take the easy way out by simply killing the project. You may be throwing away a highly profitable opportunity.

You may have had a great new product that people loved for one reason while your advertising was stressing other reasons. A few basic copy changes may be all that is needed to significantly swing the needle.

Possibly your premium price was too premium, and for 15% less, which may still make the item highly profitable, the product may be a smashing success.

■ Here are a couple of other pointers:

Don't be cheap. If there is a controversial alternative, such as a different package or different message, for a few thousand dollars more, add another cell. Besides ultimately putting the issue to rest one way or another, the extra cell can be used to validate the results in the original cell.

Listen to the results. It is quite easy to rationalize or dismiss unpopular results or even to figuratively kill the messenger. If you do, you are betting heavily against the house odds, since the major laboratory test marketing services have an excellent record of validation of past studies.

Use research—and in today's difficult climate of going from idea to marketplace, use laboratory test marketing to help you and your company do a better job in making the product on your desk a sure winner.

Do Focus Groups Work?

BY THEODORE J. GAGE

EVANSTON, ILL.—By the time a new product or advertising campaign rolls out nationally, it has generated a mountain of paperwork. There are computer printouts, presentations and thick reports on who buys, where they buy, how often and how much—quantitative information.

A successful test marketing strategy also includes qualitative information. Advertisers ask questions such as: Why do people buy a product? What do they like? Why does it meet their needs and how does it fit their life styles?

The focus group, say research specialists, is one of the best ways to obtain such useful qualitative information. The ground rules for establishing and running focus groups remain fairly consistent. The groups, which comprise members of a projected target market, average eight to 12 people. A moderator—either from the client, agency or an outside company—conducts a session lasting about two hours.

From that point on, almost everyone has a different opinion about focus groups.

"Very few people believe or will say focus groups are no good," says Bobby Calder, a professor of behavioral science in management at Northwestern University, Evanston, Ill. He has studied focus groups extensively and often moderates sessions.

"But they have been misused and often underused because so many people are afraid to deal with qualitative information. Everyone is hung up on the magic of surveys and sampling. It seems so scientific, but it isn't."

Mr. Calder argues that, although each type of research has its place, qualitative information is just as legitimate as quantitative information. "Qualitative information gathering has been a closet kind of thing in the profession," he says. "It's often used only as a stepping-stone, but it can be much more useful than that."

Marketing researchers say that where, when and how often focus groups should be used varies from case to case. Most often, however, they say the focus group should be one of the earliest steps in the marketing process, a point some would dispute.

■ "The classic approach is to view group discussion as the first step getting into a product study," says Calvin Gage, director of research at Leo Burnett Co., Chicago. "But why would its usefulness be limited? Qualitative research doesn't always have to come first."

As the marketing process advances and the information gathered gets more and more specific, the primary objective—finding out what makes the consumer buy a particular product or service—may become obscured by the volume of data. "If used judiciously," says Mr. Gage, "focus groups can be helpful when used after the quantitative gathering is over."

The key to using focus groups to their fullest is to keep an open mind about when and how often to use them, says Sharon Salling, a veteran moderator and Southwest regional director of United States Testing Co., Houston.

■ Group discussions, she explains, can be used to provide broad, general information about consumers' moods and attitudes. They can also yield useful information about specifics on pricing or packaging details. Occasionally, two sets of focus groups can prove useful—one in the pretesting stage and another after the product has entered its first test market.

"After test market introduction—especially if things aren't going well—focus groups can be used to help find out what's going wrong," says Mr. Gage. "Sometimes there are little problems that didn't show up in earlier research."

Whether or not marketers turn to focus groups often depends on how a company's research director and department feel about the usefulness of qualitative information. "Focus groups are among the most overused and abused tools we have," says Philip E. Levine, exec director of research at Ogilvy & Mather, New York.

Focus groups, he says, are useful in their proper place. But that place should usually be in the planning and idea generating stages. The qualitative information, he explains, can support quantitative studies but should never serve as a substitute for quantitative work.

■ Beyond the question of when to use the focus group, another area of contention centers on how the resulting data are interpreted. Although no one admits to doing it, the marketing experts say they are aware researchers sometimes interpret qualitative information as hard data.

"When you have eight or ten focus groups conducted in strategic areas across the country," says one veteran moderator, "it can be a tremendous temptation to say things like 'out of 100 people, x number felt this way and y number felt this way' and so on."

The temptation grows even stronger during times of inflation, says a research director, because the cost of obtaining quantitative information rises. Because running a series of focus groups can be relatively inexpensive—costing anywhere from $500 to $3,000—certain focus group results could be serving as a substitute for quantitative data. "I'm afraid the cases of misuse are increasing," he explains.

Irving S. White, president of CRA Inc., Los Angeles, and a pioneer of the focus group concept, agrees that to use qualitative information as one would use numbers is wrong.

But Mr. White, showing his enthusiasm for qualitative studies, goes further than most researchers in defining the focus group's role in test marketing. "I feel I can get more out of relating to consumers on a face-to-face basis than anyone can get out of a questionnaire. Quantitative data simply isn't valuable in development of strategy." He says he uses quantitative data as an adjunct to his qualitative work—a procedure directly opposite to that which the majority of researchers follows.

■ Obviously, the use and importance of focus groups varies as greatly as every decisionmaker's opinion on how useful qualitative information is. But anyone who uses group discussion agrees that a knowledgeable moderator and proper interpretation of the information determine how useful the results will be.

"Unfortunately, some clients only want tapes or transcripts of focus groups," says Linda Leemaster, an experienced moderator with Market Facts, Chicago. "Qualitative information really depends on how it's interpreted and correlated. I like to feel a good moderator can add some valuable insights."

William Wells, director of research at Needham, Harper & Steers, Chicago, says moderators are critical to the success of focus groups. Not only can they help analyze the discussions, but they must also lead the discussions to get participants to talk about what clients need to know.

Adds Andrew Purcell, exec vp-marketing services of Tucker Wayne & Co., Atlanta: "The moderator of a focus group must be able to spot things as he goes along. It's important that he have a very good knowledge of his subject so that he not only moderates the discussion but can also lead it."

The choice of moderator also leads to differing opinions. A manufacturer doing in-house research or the advertising agency or marketing company can either use their own moderators or hire outside people.

■ Both methods have advantages and drawbacks. "The more involved in the project the moderator is, the better able he or she is to ask the critical questions and to know what the marketing goals are," says a veteran moderator. But the in-house moderator, he says, is usually deeply involved in the project. That can be a drawback.

"It isn't an overt thing, but when you moderate a focus group, you're subjected to subtle pressures," he explains. "There's a lot of money at stake and you work for the company that stands to lose time and money if the product fails. No one is dumb enough to tell his moderator to produce certain results. It's just that if you have a vested interest in a project, it can affect your ability to interpret and analyze focus group results with some degree of objectivity."

Sharon Salling says, "It's tough to moderate a focus group, then analyze it, and tell yourself, 'I won't be influenced just because I worked on an ad.' You can't help but be influenced." Ms. Salling worked as a moderator for agencies before joining U.S. Testing.

The focus group concept is a fairly simple one and most researchers agree that it has a place in test marketing. But how, when and why it is used is as open to debate and interpretation as the information they generate.

The Quintessential Market

BY WALLY TOKARZ

ROCK ISLAND, ILL.—Blend industrial and agricultural businesses, white and blue collar workers, a population of approximately 374,500, three daily newspapers, three television stations and 10 commercial radio stations, and you have the ingredients of an attractive test market.

That's the Quad Cities, the metropolitan area made up of Davenport, Ia., and Rock Island and Moline, Ill. (the fourth city is Bettendorf, Ia.).

Although the Mississippi River, a very natural borderline, divides the area, it is still looked upon as one metropolitan center, one community. And it is a community that over recent years has served a number of manufacturers as a market for new products undergoing tests.

Amstar Co. tested its Domino liquid brown sugar here, and S. C. Johnson & Co. came to the area with its Befresh! toilet bowl deodorizer. For Swift & Co., the Quad Cities seemed the ideal place to test its Sizzlean.

■ Why has this area proved to be alluring to some test marketers? Why does it seem to be included on many lists of the nation's recommended test markets? Answers to such questions may supply some insights into the thinking that goes into test market selections.

Interviews with local media execs, manufacturers and researchers produced some of the reasons for the Quad Cities' desirability:

● Influence from outside areas is minimal. Residents of the area are served, for the most part, by the local media.

● Average household income is slightly above the national average, and the economy rests on a diversified base. Other demographic characteristics also make the area attractive.

● Facilities and retail outlets suited to test marketing functions are readily available.

● The presence of AdTel, a research company that has permanent test market facilities here, brings in various consumer goods companies. The Quad Cities is one of four locales nationwide in which AdTel has set up such facilities, the others being Peoria, Ill., Charleston, W.Va., and Bakersfield, Cal.

The initial condition—the relative media isolation—enables the Quad Cities to pass the first test of a test market.

"There is no outside influence here from either Chicago or Des Moines or any of the other larger Midwest metro markets," said Al Roels, manager of general advertising at the *Moline Daily Dispatch* and *Rock Island Argus*. "We have our own three network outlets, plus cablevision. Our newspapers are isolated. We get very little circulation from Chicago or Des Moines."

Having the three papers, according to Mr. Roels, has played a key role in the area's test marketing attractiveness. "It takes three papers to cover this market," he said, "and advertisers can actually test different copy in each of the papers at

28

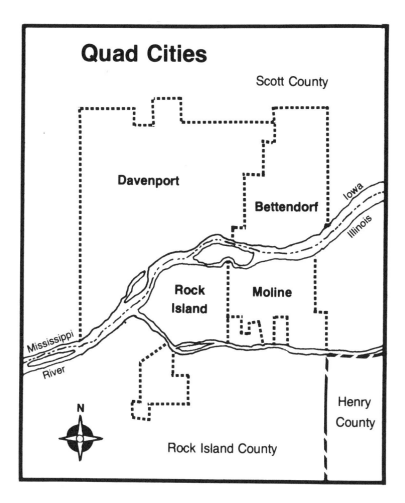

Quad Cities

Scott County

Davenport

Bettendorf

Iowa

Illinois

Rock Island

Moline

Mississippi River

N

Henry County

Rock Island County

the same time and check responses to which ad pulls he best."

■ But such a media setup would make little difference if the Quad Cities did not have the numbers—the demographics—it does. Said Harold Heath, general sales manager of WOC-TV in Davenport: "It's just a good solid market representative of midwestern America. It has a good balance between heavy industry and agriculture. Its factories have brought a relative stability of income to the area."

Underlying Mr. Heath's comments is the relative prosperity that manufacturers, such as Deere & Co. in Moline, have brought to the area. The 1978 household income averaged $21,685, making it 19th among the 100 leading U.S. markets. The figures also make the area the 39th market in the nation for effective buying income, according to Jack Bennett, vp and general manager of WHBF (am, fm) in Rock Island.

The market itself, moreover, is diverse enough to enable researchers to make projections for potential national rollouts. "The Quad Cities metropolitan market is a cosmopolitan area," said Mr. Bennett. "The labor force and service people, such as sales and insurance, is just excellent in the market."

He added that the population's average age—just over 29 years old—also makes the area attractive.

"We've been able to go through the last recession without nearly the rate of unemployment that other markets had," he said. "We've been able to have a solid growth."

That was a point Mr. Heath affirmed. "Even when automotive sales were down around the country, the Quad Cities' dealers reported last November that they were up a little," he said.

Such business activity has given the Quad Cities a retail establishment that, again, is attractive to test marketers. "The fact that we have the Eagle food center buying headquarters, Geifman Food Stores and Farm House Foods helps," said Mr. Roels of the Moline and Rock Island papers. "Most of our test items have been grocery products. We have approximately 25 food brokerage companies, plus more than 125 direct sales representatives for national companies living right here.

"So, whether they choose to go through their own sales force for test marketing and auditing stores or whether they hire outside auditers, the people that can do it are here. That's important when you're looking at test markets."

One reason there are people "here" is that the Quad Cities is a permanent test market in AdTel's stable. Both S. C. Johnson & Son and Swift & Co. indicated that AdTel was an important consideration in their decision to use the Quad Cities.

"The Quad Cities has come up because in a number of cases we've used AdTel," said Dick Chay, director of marketing research at S. C. Johnson. "The area also offers some interesting test capabilities with its cable operation."

■ Charles D. McBride, marketing research director at Swift, also pointed to AdTel's handling of the cable tv system in the area as an important factor. "We use the Quad Cities a lot because of the cable capability, which doesn't exist in very many markets," Mr. McBride said. "It's really a function of Ad-Tel. When we go into that market, we can test different levels of advertising spending or different kinds of advertising by making use of that cable."

Cable tv, according to AdTel president William McKenna, controls the distribution of the media to the local market. He said test marketers can use it along with radio and newspapers to target the message of the test brand without spill-out into other areas.

With cable, Mr. McKenna said, an advertiser can buy a spot from the local broadcasters, as well as network time. This allows the advertiser to cut into a well defined audience and substitute the network commercial with one about the new product being tested in the Quad Cities.

Still, the question remains: Why did AdTel choose the Quad Cities in the first place? The answer: For pretty much the same reason the local media execs cited.

"There are three elements that are really important in selecting test markets, and it's the whole gut of Quad Cities," said Mr. McKenna. "That's the projectability on a demographic basis, on a retail condition basis and on affluency of the population. The Quad Cities gets an 'A' in each of those three areas.

Elaborating on each point, Mr. McKenna said: "It [the area] has representative demographics, particularly representative of the large metropolitan areas of the U.S. It has the kind of young profile, working women and types of important demographics that occur in a Chicago or New York but may not occur in a Cedar Rapids or Missoula, Mont. It's out in the cornfields, but it isn't a cornfield town. That makes it unique because it has the demography of the areas where most of the population in

Amstar Co. brought its Domino liquid brown sugar to the Quad Cities for a test, while S.C. Johnson & Co. did the same for its Befresh! toilet bowl deodorizer.

the U.S. is and where you are really trying to project to."

Projectability, he said, is the "whole" thing. "If the market weren't projectable, I don't care how good we are as a market research company, we would never be successful simply because the results that we've taken from the market and extrapolated to the total U.S. would not prove to be true."

Of the retail chains, Mr. McKenna said: "You have to have most of your major retail chains, grocery and drug, well represented. All are competing just as a group of competitors in New York or Los Angeles would. So you get the retail feature ads and the tv advertising that gives it the big market type of media input.

And when they do get in the Quad Cities' media, those ads meet a lot of disposable dollars. More than half the households, said Mr. McKenna, have two or more wage earners. "That's why the retail situation there is so competitive, because there are a lot of dollars float-

ing around in the Quad Cities household. And that household, by and large, is worth a lot more money." It reflects the affluency of the population.

To explore this population and its wants, AdTel uses diary panels—a strategy Mr. McBride of Swift called "valuable"—through the services of Per-Mar Market Research in Davenport. The consumer purchase diaries are sent by mail, and participants keep track or purchases not only to find out the aggregate sales, but also how many people try and, more importantly, how many repeat their purchases.

Per-Mar also helps with telephone interviews and controlled store work, in which the company will put a product in the stores for the duration of a test so that they can talk to consumers to find out why they bought it.

AdTel, of course, is not the only market researcher to note the Quad Cities' usefulness. Dancer Fitzgerald Sample, New York, in its latest annual "Guide to Test

Market Media Planning and Market Selection," included the Quad Cities among the 46 markets recommended

"It [the area] meets the criteria that we think are important," said Ira Weinblatt, senior vp and director of media planning at DFS. "It has an adequate number of tv and radio stations that effectively cover the market from the originating market. It has good newspapers and Sunday supplements."

Mr. Weinblatt pointed out another advantage of the area: "A very important thing from our point of view as buyers of media is that the market is priced reasonably. You're getting value. There are some markets that historically have been good but they have tried to take advantage of that opportunity by jacking their prices up, specifically in the broadcast media, and they've made themselves uneconomical."

And a third thing Mr. Weinblatt—as well as AdTel—likes the Quad Cities' size. "We think there are problems if you go into a market that's very big or go to one very small," he said. "A very big one is not manageable for test marketing purposes. It's tough to get distributions. There are so many pieces to it that it may be hard to get a good reading. If it's too small, just a few who buy the product can distort the whole test."

■ AdTel, which works in markets that range from 75,000 to 150,000 homes, favors Quad Cities because it allows the company to keep costs controlled.

"It may cost as much as $20,000,000 to $50,000,000 to introduce a product nationally, depending on how large your objective is,"

Mr. McKenna said. "Well, you can't afford to risk for any company that kind of money unless you know you're going to sell. You can come into a market like Quad Cities and, when you take a look at all the costs involved, you're maybe in the area of $250,000 to $500,000 per product to run your test. So it serves the purpose of being a stand-in for a larger test area but at efficient prices."

This may all appear as if the Quad Cities is the perfect test market. There is, however, a drawback.

"The one problem we have with it is that the income is a little bit higher than we would like it to be represented," said Mr. Weinblatt. "But I think for most consumer products disposable income is not really a crucial factor. If you're testing a soap, headache remedy or toothpaste, it's not really that critical of an element. But if you're testing a high price car, then you might have another problem."

■ William McKenna may be boasting, but he stands firmly when he says: "If you put a test in our market and let us handle the media program through a combination of local broadcast and cable, make the newspaper buy and control the couponing just in the market, set up the stores just the way they would be in the total U.S., then I'll tell you, if it says that it will sell in the Quad Cities at X-dollars, that X-dollars is going to be there when you go national."

In the Quad Cities, in other words, manufacturers can create a "little America" marketing plan that's typical of the entire U.S. and manipulate the different parts of the plan at very low risk.

The Role of Local Media

BY B. G. YOVOVICH

CHICAGO—Though the primary criteria used to select test markets revolve around a locale's demographics, the quality of the local media also helps to whittle down the choices.

"The media consumption in your test marketing effort must be representative of what you will be using in the areas to which the distribution ultimately will expand," says Greg Blaine, media director in the Chicago office of Foote, Cone & Belding.

"When you do test marketing," adds Tom Schneider, vp of Burgoyne Inc., a Cincinnati-based test marketing consultant, "the test tries to reduce the real world down to a small market, and the media are an important part of this. It is important to remember that you are not only testing the product, but are testing the media weights and ad campaign that you are planning to use as well."

Perhaps the most widely discussed test market characteristic is the extent to which a market enjoys "media isolation" and particularly the amount of "spill-out" of local media and the "spill-in" from outside sources.

Spill-out is undesirable because "advertising in areas in which the product is not available" can provoke customer ill will, explains Ira Weinblatt, senior vp of Dancer Fitzgerald Sample, New York.

Cost problems can also arise.

"The cost of producing the product generally is the most significant part of the test marketing budget," says Arthur Oken, president of New York-based ParaTest Marketing, "and if the spillage out is such that 40% of your product has to go out of the test area, this can get pretty expensive. Sometimes, you may not even have enough product to be able to do this."

If the product is extremely limited, spillage out problems may require that ads identify where the product is available.

■ Spillage in problems can be even more significant than spillage out.

"Media campaigns from other cities can affect the research that you're trying to do in your test," explains Mr. Schneider of Burgoyne. "If a competitor spends X dollars in Peoria, for example, but 10X in Chicago, it's tough to measure how much of that spills into your test in Peoria and what effect it has on your results."

"If an area gets 30% to 40% spillage in," says Mr. Oken of ParaTest, the spillage corrupts the data obtained so extensively that "you can't consider it for use as a test market."

Because of the population density and media saturation that characterize the region, "spillage of both kinds is a big problem in the Northeast," says Mr. Oken. "Portland, Me., is the only market in the Northeast that you can go in unless you decide to go with at least 20% spillage. That's why such [relatively isolated] areas as Phoenix-Tucson are so popular."

Media availability is also an important consideration in the selection of a market.

"A test market must be typical in number and balance of media outlets," says Mr. Weinblatt, whose agency annually puts out a comprehensive "Test Market Guide." "If you are using tv, you want to have at least three tv stations. If you are using radio, you don't want a market in which one station dominates, because it doesn't happen that way in the real world."

"If your national campaign will be heavy in late night media," says Mr. Blaine of FCB, "you wouldn't want to test in the mid-U.S. before moving your distribution to Los Angeles and New York."

On the print side, because newspaper availability for the most part does not vary significantly from market to market, it is generally not a factor in deciding on a test market location. Magazines, however, can be a very different story.

■ "Often you can buy the magazine you want," says Mr. Weinblatt of DFS. "Most women's magazines, for example, have great test market flexibility, and, if you are a major corporate client, you can actually cut the test market advertising in on your national program (for other products). Organizations such as Magazine Network Inc., which sells space within certain market areas, are also available."

In the cases in which scaled-down versions of the magazines to be used in the national campaign are not available, test marketers are forced to look for areas that have local alternatives, such as newspaper Sunday supplements.

This can cause availability of magazine alternatives to become important in test market selection.

A final consideration is media cost.

"Some markets have taken advantage of their popularity as test markets," says Mr. Weinblatt, and have increased their ad rates significantly. Mr. Weinblatt points to Seattle and Phoenix as areas in which media costs "have been too high," although he says that sometimes these trends "turn around and straighten themselves out."

Mr. Oken of ParaTest downplays the role of cost in market selection.

■ "You should try to translate the reach and frequency of your advertising campaign to the test market, rather than trying to translate the budget cost," says Mr. Oken. "If you're planning a $1,000,000 national campaign, you shouldn't plan to spend $10,000 on advertising for a 1% market test" because that probably will not be enough to give you a representative reach and frequency.

Important as media considerations are in deciding where to locate a market, there are times when all this concern is completely irrelevant.

"In one case, our client was only interested in finding out if he could sell the product to the trade," recalls Mr. Blaine of FCB. "In this instance, the actual media schedules were not important so the local media situation was not important.

"It all depends on what you want to read" into your test.

Getting There—First

BY B. G. YOVOVICH

ROCHESTER, N.Y.—The companies that supplied coffee to the Rochester, N.Y., market could smell something brewing. A top Procter & Gamble officer who had been working in P&G's western coffee operations had been spotted in the Rochester area.

Rival companies supplying coffee to the area went on alert. The officer's activity, they concluded, signaled either the early stages of a market test of a new coffee product or a full-scale assault on the local coffee market by P&G. In either case, a counteroffensive was in order.

Within days, and before P&G could get its product through the distribution network and onto the shelves, the competition laid down a barrage of cents-off coupons that eventually blunted much of the P&G effort.

■ "I see it happen all the time," says Arthur Oken, president of ParaTest Marketing, White Plains, N.Y., "especially in the grocery store areas with the largest shelving, such as detergents, coffee and pet food."

It is just one of the problems that can occur in goods distribution, one of the key components of the test marketing process.

Most companies in highly competitive product categories keep their salesmen on the lookout for new products appearing on the grocery store shelves.

By getting an early enough warning, companies can take advantage of the distribution delays that create lags between the first appearance of the product and the time it achieves sufficient market penetration to begin the market test.

"Sometimes it can take two months to build up to 70% distribution by using the normal channels of distribution," says Tom Schneider, vp of Burgoyne Inc., a Cincinnati-based test marketing company.

■ When a company discovers that a competitor is about to begin a market test, often it will try to pry information about the test from the local media.

"Suppose a salesman from company A comes across a new soap from company B on a grocery store shelf," says Gerald Szorek, national ad manager of the Times Publishing Co. in Erie, Pa., one of the nation's most popular test marketing locations.

"Company A knows that within six to eight weeks, the media campaign and market test will begin, so very often they'll come to me and, in a way, try to bribe me by saying, 'We'd like to run an ad schedule with your paper if you can have it run the same time that company B is running its ads.'

"Of course, I can't do that since it would be telling company A when their competition is going to be running ads, which is against our policy," says Mr. Szorek.

■ Competitive disruptions aside, problems with the standard channels of distribution can cause test marketers other headaches as well.

As store buying committees rely more and more on computer analysis to make buying and facing decisions, for example, the individual store manager has less leeway in making decisions about new products. Resistance to new products, as a result, has been increasing in recent years.

Even when the product overcomes this barrier and is accepted by buying committees, if the local distribution network serves an area much larger than the given test market, significant "product spillage" out of the testing area can result. Because many new products are manufactured in expensive special runs, this spillage can be very costly.

In an effort to avoid such problems, many companies are turning to "controlled" distribution for their market tests.

Instead of using the company's own sales force to set up the test, the controlled test employs an outside agency to guarantee distribution.

The agency, in effect, rents shelf space from the stores involved in the test, sells the products to the store on consignment, and, using its own fleet of vehicles and personnel, takes responsibility for stocking shelves, arranging product facings and performing audits.

■ "We can have the product on the shelf in three days" via controlled distribution, says Burgoyne's Mr. Schneider. This makes it possible for the marketers to begin advertising and promotion within two weeks after the "sell-in" instead of waiting the 60 to 90 days it generally takes to go through regular distribution channels.

Because the agency's personnel are directly responsible for stocking and facing the product on the store shelves, controlled distribution also enables the test marketer

to do more highly refined testing. The test marketer, for example, can have the agency vary the facings and see what result this has on the tests.

The tester can also experiment with various advertising and promotion strategies to determine which works best. In cities such as Erie, where the daily newspaper offers four zoned editions, test marketers have run a four-color ad with no coupon in one zone, a one-color ad with a 25¢ coupon in the second, a black and white ad with a 50¢ coupon in the third and, in the fourth, a $2 refund with proof of purchase. In such cases, researchers are able to compare the ads' pulling power.

Controlled distribution tests have the final advantage that, because the product goes through the controlled distribution agency rather than usual channels, the test results do not show up on figures from SAMI (Selling Areas-Marketing Inc.). This makes it more difficult for competitors to monitor the results of the test.

■ Controlled distribution can have one disadvantage: It is too good.

"The controlled distribution situation is artificial," says Vern Churchill, exec vp of Chicago-based Marketest. "Because it doesn't depend at all on the normal sales force [and is assured optimal shelf space, stocking and facings], the product is sold under more ideal conditions" than will be found in the real world.

This means that there is an upward bias in the test results obtained from a controlled distribution test. But, Mr. Churchill points out, "If the product does not achieve the sales goals that you set prior to the test, at least you know it is not because of distribution problems."

Delivering The Goods — Profile of Burgoyne

BY CYNTHIA HARDIE

CINCINNATI—"Businessmen often value their own judgment and experience entirely too much. They also often demand too simple a report and unqualified conclusions when they use market research."

Reported in ADVERTISING AGE on Feb. 23, 1953, this critical observation was made by John Burgoyne Jr., the late founder of what is now Burgoyne Inc., headquartered here.

What Mr. Burgoyne was talking about to his Philadelphia audience 27 years ago was the lack of sophistication in the use of market research, and the potential he saw for its use in the future. Since that time, business and the research industry have grown up hand in hand, with Mr. Burgoyne's company participating as a leader in the industry.

■ Today, according to Ed Brent, executive vp and board chairman of Burgoyne, the growth of the marketing research profession within corporations and agencies is not a threat but an advantage "because you no longer have to explain the need for research."

Burgoyne began in 1940 as Burgoyne Grocery and Drug Index. For many years, it was best known for its annual study, still published but now every other year, on supermarket shoppers' buying habits.

Burgoyne is now a full-service custom-research house. Because it is privately owned, no figures on sales are given, said vp Tom Schneider, but he placed the company in the top 20. The active client list in 1979 numbered 135, with the

Burgoyne Inc. specializes in minimarket test services.

largest accounts being Procter & Gamble, Kroger, Campbell Soup, Pillsbury, Ore-Ida, Colgate, Sara Lee, Kraft, Sohio, Clorox and Star-Kist, to name a few.

Services of the company are divided into two areas—sales research and consumer research, with the former making up 65% to 70% of the business. Sales research is essentially broken down into three services—standard audit, control store tests and distribution checks.

■ With 150 employes, Burgoyne also has offices in White Plains, N.Y., and San Francisco and can reach into 300 markets for field auditing, according to Mr. Schneider. This is accomplished through its subsidiary, Field-A-Test, which is one of the industry's largest task forces for in-store field work.

Burgoyne pioneered controlled store testing in the 1950s and later the minimarket test—in which the research companies contract with stores to force distribution—for which it is well known. The company's promotional brochure says: "The minimarket test has evolved into one of American package goods marketers' most valued tools for predicting new performance. Burgoyne pioneered this product forecast technique—even named it. And we've conducted more large-scale minimarket tests in more cities than any other research company in the nation."

For its consumer research, Burgoyne maintains a WATS telephone center. A network of local telephone representatives is also available in markets for localized research. Burgoyne is widely known, too, for personal consumer interviewing, which was the basis for its supermarket study when women were interviewed door to door.

A reflection of the changing times, Mr. Schneider said, is that door-to-door interviewing is seldom used now and to reach the consumer by phone means making phone calls after 5 p.m. The company says it has grown up with suburban shopping malls and has a nationwide network of malls "to provide the ideal environment for intercept interviewing."

Mr. Brent, the exec vp, pointed to the steady evolution in hardware that keeps the company on top of the heap of data that comes through its computer center. Burgoyne staffers also design all software.

■ The challenge, Mr. Brent said, is to eliminate errors. Now the staff is working on a program for a "double computer edit"; that is, a process by which the computer will not accept data that is not congruous. For example, Mr. Brent said, shopping at a Safeway store in Cincinnati would be impossible so such data would be rejected.

Burgoyne maintains a complete tape library, which Mr. Brent calls unique for a custom house, so clients can refer back to their own research studies.

In the testing stages now is a plan to use scanner data so product movement can be read as it happens, Mr. Schneider said. As more stores institute the scanner checkouts, diary panels can be used with the scanner. This would provide a computer printout of everything a diary participant bought at that store and would leave him or her free of having to write down all purchases.

The disadvantage, Mr. Schneider said, is that sole reliance on the scanner data would "lose" every item the shopper purchased at another store. So, he said, "right now, we're testing the test."

Trying Too Hard—Mistakes That Make A Loser

BY GREG SPAGNA

NEW YORK—Sometimes it helps to pay more attention to paying less attention. That's true, at least, in test marketing.

In fact, paying too much attention has been one of the most common errors to afflict the field.

You might think you have avoided such errors in the past, but don't be too hasty.

The list of errors and misguided efforts that follow, including "over-attention," are committed by all of us: Every major manufacturer of consumer products, every advertising agency and every research company dealing with the test marketing of new products has been guilty. The degree of fault may vary somewhat among the three groups, but it is there to be shared by all.

After 12 years of test marketing and after exposure to 140 new product test markets in the past three years alone, I am amazed how some mistakes keep recurring. These errors cut across all major product categories—food, drug, apparel, hard goods and related consumer products. Moreover, the manufacturers and agencies of these products are both big and small, sophisticated and non-sophisticated.

■ The forces that contribute to these errors are most often not a function of incompetence. Rather,

Greg Spagna is president of Market Facts in New York.

they might be classified under the dubious heading of "trying to execute a perfect test market."

Corporate management contributes with its sometimes blind desire to come out with new successful products (the cornerstone of any good company).

Product management contributes with its desire to "uncover every detail" (which is not a bad philosophy since most new product managers are evaluated on their performance and not on the performance of the brand when national introduction rolls around).

Ad agencies contribute with their desire to serve; thus, national-to-test-market translations are designed to reach as many households as possible.

Finally, research departments (and research companies) contribute with their desire to be associated with a winner (no one applauds test market research that kills products).

■ The point is: We have encountered a number of common mistakes in the test marketing of an enormous number of new products for virtually every major company in the U.S. Our goal is to improve the "state of the art."

If there is one thing we have found, it is that test marketing is not a science and it never will be. It is an art, and because of that, its subtleties become very important and can be overlooked in an attempt to do "a perfect job."

The most common mistakes in test marketing are listed below. The first three, in our judgment, account for better than three out of four product failures (that is, products successful in test market but not nationally).

1. "Over-attention." This is by far the biggest problem in test marketing today. You may argue that you can never pay enough attention to setting up a test market. However, one should not confuse paying attention with over-attention.

Over-attention is geared only to making the product a success, not to finding out if it is a success. Over-attention is personal visits by brand people to tell the field force and the trade of the specialness and importance of the new product. Over-attention is the spending of unusual amounts of time to making the product more available and more "pretty." Over-attention is special efforts by the ad agency to secure test markets that have excellent tv coverage (which may or may not be representative of tv coverage).

Over-attention is the extra care by the research staff to sampling consumers who are guaranteed to live within distribution areas of the product (which may result in the selection of those who live closer than average).

Experience has shown us that over-attention makes many products perform better in test market than nationally. It is not surprising that only 40% of all new products that pass through successful test markets are also successful nationally.

The best way to overcome the problem of over-attention is to charge someone at brand level to be the devil's advocate. It would be his responsibility to see that things are carried out at "normal" or "average" levels. He would ask the question: "Can I duplicate this marketing action in McAllenphar, Tex.?"

2. Incorrect volume forecasts. One of the most difficult aspects of test marketing is correctly forecasting introductory and going

year volume. This problem is unavoidable because we use one, two or even four markets to predict national performance. Research, however, often compounds the problem by using only one method of forecasting—share of market, or unit or dollar sales. Additionally, research fails to make adequate adjustments for distribution levels, category development indexes (CDI) and the like.

In the case of controlled test marketing, adjustments (which in some cases may vary from 15% to 50%) are mandatory. It has been our experience, as well as our clients', that volume forecasts of test products are generally overstated rather than understated—even for products that are successful nationally.

The way to limit forecasting errors is first to be somewhat pessimistic in your approach (or have low, as well as high, estimates) and second to use several different methods of forecasting.

Don't use only audits. Repeat rates, so important to a product's success, can come only from consumers. Telephone tracking studies or diaries are almost a must to guarantee accurate forecasting.

Lastly, there is the need for adjustments. If you are making forecasts without making adjustments, you are making forecasts incorrectly.

3. Establishing unrealistic in-store conditions. This most frequently committed error in test marketing refers to achieving in-store conditions that can never be matched on a national basis—extra facings, greater percentage of displays, eye-level stocking, etc.

The brand manager sets his facings of the product by the market leader (which may have taken ten years to achieve its facings). Sometimes he consults his field force and they tell him exactly what he wants to hear: Five facings in a three facing category, or 40% displays where the category calls for 15%.

The comedy of the situation is that the field force does exactly what it proposed to do—in test market. When the product goes national, three facings are what the product attains. While there is no solution to this problem, being wary and somewhat pessimistic about what the field force says it can attain may better help you set realistic conditions.

4. Incorrect media translations. This does not happen often, but when it does it is devastating. When a product achieves a 90% awareness level and a 35% trial level in Month 1, don't jump up and down for joy; go see what you did wrong. More than likely it is an incorrect national-to-test-market translation.

When national media plans call for magazine advertising and test markets don't have magazines, don't let the agency substitute tv advertising dollars for magazine advertising dollars—they're not the same. Remember, ad agencies want to do a good job in setting up the media plan for test marketing. On the media plan, all we really want is a normal job.

5. Changing objectives after the results are in. This error is more widespread than commonly realized. It happens with those marginal new products—you know, the ones that almost reach volume forecasts, the ones hard to let go.

Here, the brand manager adjusts advertising budgets ($6,000,000 to $4,000,000, for instance) and promotional schedules (20% couponing to 10% couponing) and tells the ad agency to direct copy at a more valuable market segment. The end result is that the brand manager shows corporate management that he still can reach profit goals on smaller volume.

Our experience says: Baloney! Test market the product longer under the new marketing plan with new objectives. Don't change the rules of the game after it has started.

6. Selection of the wrong test markets. Selection of the wrong test markets has been going on since the advent of test marketing. Test marketing an orange juice concentrate in Florida or California, a soap in Cincinnati, or an antihistamine in Phoenix are incorrect market selections. Wrong market selection is not a common problem, but the best way to control it is to test in more than one market and pay careful attention to market characteristics.

7. Failure to take into consideration the atypicality of test markets. This is not to be confused with the selection of wrong markets. Category development, brand development, shopper characteristics, etc., are the things sometimes overlooked. Selecting a market with a high CDI may be a correct choice, but volume forecasts should take into consideration just how high the CDI is.

8. Assuming competitive environment will be the same nationally as it was in test market. Many products we have tested are for new categories or are unique to existing categories. Thus, the success of your product might be a forecast of the success of the category. As competitive "me-too" products come in, sharing of the category takes place naturally.

Volume forecasting of products of this type should have fallback positions to take into consideration different competitive scenarios. This can protect against overspending in advertising and promotions so that product profits can still be maintained with somewhat lower volumes.

9. Failure to conduct consumer research. This is somewhat related to the volume forecasting error. It involves carrying out a test market with only audit data; awareness of the product, advertising recall, attitudes and images of the product, trial and repeat rates all go unmeasured. All that is necessary to correct this problem is to carry out consumer research in conjunction with the audits.

10. Insufficient attention. This usually infrequent error occurs when a brand manager assumes something is being done. He assumes that the ad agency is reviewing consumer characteristics of a possible test market. He assumes that the field force is operating normally and not excessively. Forgetting the words "I assumed" in planning a test market usually corrects this problem.

These then are the errors we have encountered most often in test marketing. But if I had to suggest just one reminder, it would be to urge corporate management to make sure test marketing is carried out as its name implies—as a *test*, to determine if a new product is a profitable business venture.

It is not a conscientious effort by a determined team (all of us included) to try to guarantee success. Rather, "smart" decisions should be made to allow the product an opportunity for success—the same opportunity it will have when it is launched nationally.

On-Air Scores Don't Tell All

BY SONIA YUSPEH
AND ARTHUR J. KOVER

NEW YORK—Your commercial scores a 28 in an on-air recall test. Happy days. You've got a winner.

Another commercial scores 18. Groans and moans. You've got a loser.

But is that really the case? Recent evidence indicates that the 28 may not be a winner. Why? *Because program environment invalidates on-air recall scores.*

This is not the only charge against on-air testing. For years, conscientious researchers have had trouble with this form of testing. There have been a variety of reasons raised as to why on-air is a flawed attempt to measure what commercials do. Many researchers have pointed out that specific test scores are often unstable, that day-after recall taps only a small part of what a commercial does to viewers, that the seeming security of an on-air recall score may conceal many kinds of uncontrolled variations in the testing situation.

■ And yet on-air sails along. Major campaigns for corporate giants live or die when an on-air report comes in. Why? Partly because it

makes a kind of intuitive sense to use on-air.

After all, aren't we measuring responses of real people watching real programs in their homes? Isn't it comforting to be able to depend on one simple number rather than having to grapple with a whole set of statistics covering the multifaceted aspects of a commercial's performance? Isn't it helpful to have nice, clear norms that tell us whether we're doing well or badly?

These appeals of on-air testing are highly seductive. But a recent study of program environments done by J. Walter Thompson Co., New York, raises serious questions about just what on-air measures.

The JWT project suggests that specific program contexts strongly distort on-air test scores.

The Thompson researchers, in collaboration with six leading advertisers who jointly sponsored the research, used a complex study design of six commercials. Each commercial was exposed 12 times on the air: Two times in each of three "R" type programs and two times in each of three "Q" type programs.

("R" and "Q" represent two very different kinds of programing. We can't identify them further except to say that one program type was perceived by the public to be relatively violent, the other not.)

The day after the exposure, qualified viewers were questioned about brand recall, playback of elements of the commercial, buying intent and perceptions of the brand advertised. (By the way, the most common on-air question-

Sonia Yuspeh is Senior vp-Research & Planning at J. Walter Thompson, New York. Arthur J. Kover, is Research Development Director at J. Walter Thompson, New York.

Table 1

BRAND RECALL

SIX COMMERCIALS FOR SIX PRODUCTS

| | Averaged by Program Type | | Range of Recall Scores | |
	3 "R" Shows	3 "Q" Shows	Low (Show)	(High) (Show)
Commercial #1	104	96	80 (Q-1)	115 (R-2)
Commercial #2	96	103	83 (Q-3)	128 (Q-1)
Commercial #3	99	101	85 (R-3)	125 (R-2)
Commercial #4	103	97	78 (R-1)	120 (R-2)
Commercial #5	97	103	78 (R-1)	117 (Q-1)
Commercial #6	100	100	88 (R-1)	117 (R-2)

(Note: 100 is the over-all average recall score for each commercial. Codes in parentheses designate specific programs in which recall scores were achieved.)

---

naires don't include the last two items.)

The study design was aimed at examining program effects ("R" and "Q") on commercial performance, an issue that has long been important. Usually major services deal with it by averaging results from programs of a similar type. When this is done, there is no difference, on the average, between commercials embedded in, say, police programs and the same commercials in situation comedies.

■ This was true, too, for the commercials in this test. Looking at each commercial as averaged over the three "R" and three "Q" programs, there were no important differences in the performance of each commercial.

But that wasn't enough. After all, commercials are generally tested in the context of one specific program—not in several at one time and then averaged. When we looked at commercial performance in specific programs, the stability provided by averaging collapsed.

There were wide variations in the performance of the same com-

mercials when looked at separately in the context of individual shows. In short, we found that the same commercial can get radically different recall (and other) scores from different shows even when these shows are of the same type.

Table 1 shows the ranges and kinds of differences we found in recall scores. We went far beyond normal practices to ensure that the test samples were well matched, so we have strong reason to believe that these differences were *not* because of internal instabilities in the research. On the contrary, the evidence is compelling that the variations in commercial performance were due to specific program contexts.

In fact, because we recruited viewers to watch the designated shows and exposed the commercials twice (instead of the single exposure common to on-air testing), we would actually expect greater stability from our test, compared with normal on-air practices. If anything, the test probably understates the degree of instability in standard on-air measurements.

The instability we found was not limited to recall. Table 2 shows the total range of measurements signi-

Table 2

TYPES OF COMMERCIAL SCORES AFFECTED BY SPECIFIC SHOWS

	Brand Recall	Playback
Commercial # 1	X	X
Commercial # 2	X	X
Commercial # 3	X	X
Commercial # 4	X	X
Commercial # 5	X	X
Commercial # 6	X	X

		Brand Perceptions		
	Buying Intent	A	B	C
Commercial # 1	X	X	X	X
Commercial # 2		X	X	
Commercial # 3	X	X	X	
Commercial # 4	X	X		X
Commercial # 5	X	X	X	
Commercial # 6				X

ficantly affected by specific program context. This chart shows that, in most cases, the specific program environment influenced *all* of the measurements of effectiveness tested.

And, even though the chart doesn't show it, the program environment moved these measurements all over the map. That is, even for the same commercial, a specific program would move one measurement (say, recall) one way and another one (say, buying intent) another way.

The evidence is clear:

• **On-air testing is risky.** Unless you test each commercial in several shows and average the results, you run the risk of seriously misreading the effectiveness of your commercial. It may be better than you think—or worse—depending on the show in which you test it. And there is no sure way of ferreting out the influence of the show (except by averaging across several shows).

• **Recall alone is not an adequate measure of commercial performance.** This study reinforces the work done by many other researchers that demonstrates the inadequacy of recall as a sole criteria for judging a commercial. We covered many measures of commercial performance, and we found a high degree of variability among them. The implication clearly is that commercials should not be judged solely on recall.

Burke Scores—A Measure, But A Limited Measure

BY TOM WATTS

CHICAGO—"Come to breakfast with a sock in your mouth and you're going to make an impression. But are you going to persuade anyone else to do it?"

That's J. Walter Thompson Co. research director William Hull's assessment of the test effectiveness of the sort of day-after-exposure tv commercial tests provided by Burke Research and other on-air sampling organizations.

What Mr. Hull means is that Burke-type commercial evaluations give clients a solid grasp of the intrusiveness (recall) of a given spot, but go wide of the mark in measuring the persuasiveness of the same commercial.

■ "I've found no correlation at all between recall and persuasion" in such on-air tests, he says.

Mr. Hull says JWT's Chicago clients generally do not engage in widespread Burke-type tests, preferring tracking studies that rely on telephone checks before and after commercials are run. These, he says, are "real world" measurements of both product perception and intention to buy, as opposed to simple exposure.

Ad agency creative directors and account people tend not to want to be quoted when quizzed about on-air tests of their tv commercials, but when granted anonymity they toss around phrases such as "being cursed with Burke" and firm convictions that such tests are "totally inadequate" as measuring devices.

Thompson's Mr. Hull is less reticent than some.

"My personal opinion," he says, "is that Burke tests are easy [for clients] to understand, but while they can be a fair measure of brand or product awareness, they're nowhere on viewer intention-to-use [a product]. And isn't *that* what we're trying to determine?"

There is a large—and apparently growing—body of opinion among agency (if not client) researchers that the medium does indeed affect the message in such on-air tests of marketing effectiveness. In other words, the tv show during which a commercial is shown can make an impact that will not necessarily be repeated when the same commercial is plopped into a different kind of program.

"It's quite possible—and quite common—to 'buy' a good Burke score," says a research executive for a major agency. "A great deal depends on which show you pick, and a great deal of program selection depends on what you're trying to prove—and to whom.

"Obviously," the exec adds, "your commercial will impact more on a sex-and-violence type of show than on a program by the Boston Pops."

Not all agency researchers agree.

While almost all of those surveyed have reservations about commercial tests such as Burke's (telephone calls within 24 hours of the airing of a commercial in a given market), many say the greatest drawback in such testing is that clients—and sometimes agency research chiefs—rely too much on the test results.

"Like all market tests," says Marshall Zandell of N W Ayer's Chicago office, "such [Burke-type] tests are a measure—one limited measure—of a commercial's—or a campaign's—effectiveness.

"A high Burke score is considered to be good, a low one is bad," he says, "but in terms of future effectiveness, that's not necessarily so."

Mr. Zandell says Burke-type tests are "only limited measurements, not predictions, because they measure only recall. A commercial may be intrusive, but not necessarily effective."

And Mr. Zandell, like most agency researchers, has his own scale of values in assessing commercial tests. He says Burke-type testing is "useful when properly used, but these tests are only *some* of the factors to be considered in evaluation—I give them a rather low priority."

■ Still, Mr. Zandell doesn't put down the Burke people or the usefulness of their tests. "The significance of any commercial testing project is to determine whether it communicates the message you want to deliver to the people you're trying to reach," he says. "After all, Preparation H commercials can be expected to appeal only to sufferers, and when they do that, they've done their job."

Mr. Zandell doesn't say so, but it seems probable that a Preparation H ad might "Burke-out" at a fairly low score, yet still be a solid, persuasive, hard-selling motivator to its selected market.

It's the old rifle shot vs. shotgun analogy—and Burke tests, like many other pretests, are considered better at measuring general audience scattergun campaigns than those aimed at selected audience segments.

Ad-Tel, one of the marketing services arms of Booz, Allen & Hamilton, purports to go a giant stride beyond pretesting—at a substantially greater expenditure of time and money.

Bill McKenna, a Booz, Allen & Hamilton partner and Ad-Tel's president, says his company's in-market tests, which include print ads as well as video commercials, indicate a campaign's probable effect on product sales, as opposed to viewer awareness or attitudes. The difference, he contends, is great—if not enormous.

Still, Mr. McKenna refuses to criticize Burke, Gallup, Tele-Research and others in the pretesting and on-air testing field.

■ "Such tests measure what they purport to measure," he says. "The question is: Is that sufficient to predict sales-benefit as a basis for final judgment by client or agency?"

As Mr. McKenna explains it, Ad-Tel's controlled market tests involve ad campaigns already pretested either in lab groups or on air. Often, he says, Ad-Tel will test a new campaign against an already existing, and often effective, creative strategy. And, about as often, he'll put two test approaches against each other in an effort to pin down which approach is most likely to succeed.

For instance, says Mr. McKenna, "Let's say an agency and its client map a whole new marketing strategy which is under consideration as a possible replacement for a current campaign. They're going to ask themselves whether they really should change horses.

"Maybe sales are up, and the current campaign gets its fair share of the credit. The client's going to ask why he should tinker with a formula that seems to be working. Still, he wants to widen his share of market. That's when we're called in."

Ad-Tel's clients include about half of the nation's top 100 consumer package goods producers, and the company claims to have conducted some 300-plus tests-after-pretests in the past decade.

Most pretests are pretty reliable, Mr. McKenna believes. He says trouble erupts when the results are improperly weighted during the decision-making process. Take them for exactly what they are—indicators of impact and attitudes—and they're useful.

"The difference—and it's a major one—is that we track buy, not just intent to buy," he says.

UPC Symbol Hasn't Delivered

BY EUGENE POMERANCE

CHICAGO—Ballyhooed for years as the wave of the future for all marketing measurements, checkout scanners today are just making ripples. And for test marketing grocery store products they're still all promise—no performance.

It's true scanners are revolutionary. They're good. Even great. But they're not really the equivalent of 1776 or 1984. The revolution is really only in the cost of measuring product movement at the store level.

Scanners are supposed to measure everything that passes the checkout and record it in the store's computer. Thus it's possible to develop weekly or daily—potentially even hourly—records of product movement and to get the results soon after.

Frequent, fast, complete, no human error. That's why the use of scanners has been called a "revolution—after decades of dreaming.

"It is acclaimed as the most powerful weapon in the entire arsenal," providing "information never before possible to obtain." And it is able, the claim goes, to provide the "ratio between sales and shoppers . . . a new statistic" and "record what products join what others in a single customer's cart."

Old El Paso chiles

Betty Crocker frosting mix

Minute Maid lemonade mix

Eugene Pomerance is Senior vp-Marketing Services for Foote, Cone & Belding in Chicago.

■ But we've always been able to get weekly store audit data and get the results fast. The Toni Co. did it more than a quarter century ago. We've always been able to calculate movement per hundred customers and measure what combination of products shoppers are buying. The difference now is that we're able to get those kinds of data quite inexpensively.

What's curious to me, however, is that the real breakthrough scanners can represent has been largely overlooked: Their ability to provide a mechanized consumer purchase diary. With some makes of scanners today—and probably all makes in due course—each transaction can be identified with the customer involved.

A plastic card or simply a keyed-in number at the checkout tells the computer to store that transaction data with the customer file. That's not just less expensive—that's new. That substitutes machine recordkeeping for people recordkeeping—and that's revolutionary.

It's not without its problems—the principal one being completeness, as customers forget to hand in their card or choose to go to a store that isn't part of the system. But it does promise to be a significant advance in that kind of marketing research.

■ For store audit work, scanners are simply less expensive; they really can't do anything that hasn't been done before. Their weaknesses are different, but not really better or worse than the ones we've had with manual audits or computerized warehouse withdrawals. For consumer diary work, however, they represent something we could not do before at all.

The big research companies are pursuing the diary idea now, partly because consumer panels are often used in test marketing. And they're experimenting with scanners for store audit work.

So the researchers are ready. Marketers are ready. But for test marketing, the scanners aren't ready. And it may be a long, long time before they really are.

The problem is that there aren't enough scanner equipped stores, the right kinds of stores, in any market. Not all chains and voluntary groups are buying the machines. Even when they do, the scanners tend to be installed in the largest stores.

We may never see scanners in the mom and pop stores; marketing researchers can live with that. But it could be a long time before we see enough scanners in the smaller chains and groups—and in the smaller stores of the chains and groups that have them—to give us enough confidence in the representativeness of the store sample. Even 40% of a market isn't enough, if it's the 40% done by big stores in big store neighborhoods.

■ Well, then, if not yet for test markets, how are scanners being used?

We all know marketing data are really a secondary purpose of the scanners. Principally out of a desire for operating efficiency, grocery

Heritage House pears

Ideal flat bread

trade groups approved the concept of the Universal Product Code (UPC) in 1971, and adopted the actual numbering system in 1973. More than 90% of dry groceries are coded with those black bars, and several hardware manufacturers are trying to sell the scanners. Yet today, more than five years later, only about 500 stores have them.

Grocers so far have been looking for the "hard" savings before laying out $100,000 or more to equip each store. The hard savings originally were thought to be expected from three kinds of labor: Price marking (a saving not allowed in some states and cities), ringing up the price and bagging (the checkout person does it with the hand not being used to punch the register).

A major saving that has been added to the calculations is a reduction of what is euphemistically called shrinkage (for example, by measuring how much bread and soda the direct delivery people really did put into the store, or by discouraging the checker from "underrings").

■ While the grocers are reckoning their hard savings, several research groups have been developing data collection and processing systems:

1. The Advertising Research Foundation (ARF) foresaw the value of scanners and conducted a major pilot study in 1977 in Kansas City to determine feasibility and to develop systems.

2. The Newspaper Advertising Bureau (NAB) also saw the possibilities. NAB now gets weekly data from about 60 stores in about 14 markets, and it sells the information to manufacturers who may have various kinds of advertising and promotion experiments going on in those cities. NAB also shares the data with cooperating retailers who may have their own experiments.

3. The Tele-Research Co. can get data from three chains in five markets. They're developing test procedures for manufacturers, and they, too, are developing computer software for grocers to use to develop their own measurements of experiments.

4. Selling Areas-Marketing Inc. (SAMI) is the big supplier of computer generated figures on product movement out of the warehouses into retail stores. It was involved in the ARF experiment and expects to be ready soon to offer a scanner service to all comers.

5. Nielsen is the big supplier of standard store audits in the grocery field. The company, like SAMI, is busy developing systems to use scanners, because scanners in a practical sense could well make "regular" store audits and warehouse withdrawal data obsolete.

6. Rumors have other companies gearing up for this service, too, but there can't be many. A questionnaire mailed to every research company—about 300 of them—that lists itself in the Marketing Research Assn. directory as available to do store audits turned up only seven that said they can produce data directly from one or more stores' computers. There were a few who said they might if someone gave them an order.

7. Ralphs grocery chain in California is the reputed leader in using the data for merchandising decisions, but some independents may really be ahead on these "soft" uses. Independent computer software houses are getting involved.

■ None of the work has been in test marketing. To date, all of the experiments, tests, trials and case histories are of marketing experiments. For example, advertising amounts and time, advertising media, manufacturer promotions and retailer deals, direct mail samples vs. coupons, long-term price elasticity and retail price features, shelf location in the store and special displays and neighborhood differences have been studied.

Not without problems, either. It's nice to think of scanner data as being perfect—no human errors. It isn't so, of course. There are problems with the scanner-computer hardware, problems with product packages and printing, problems with grocery store help and with what is and is not UPC coded and problems with voids in what scanners can ever measure. Some examples:

The scanners, like all computers, have their "down" time. If you miss half of a Saturday's sales records, more than a little of the credibility of the record is lost.

In some makes of scanners, the host computer can't interrogate the store level computer by telephone lines; instead, a disk or tape cassette must be sent to the host computer location for processing and that makes daily records impractical.

■ The scanners don't always work on dented cans or crushed packages or waxy cartons. And they don't work yet on newspaper coupons because it's not practical to put UPC symbols on newsprint.

Checkers often prefer to leave big bulky packages such as 25 lbs. of dog food, or heavy items such as soft drinks, in the shopping carts and not pass them over the scanners. Case sales to restaurants or to clubs are sometimes not recorded, and shoplifted merchandise never is.

Most meat and produce, many health and beauty aid items and a lot of the other nongrocery items are not UPC coded at all.

Out-of-stock items and the number of facings a product has on the grocery store shelves can't, of course, be measured by a checkout scanner.

There is one other—apparently far more troublesome—problem reported by those involved with the system to date—too much data.

Weekly, sometimes daily, records of movement of each size of each flavor of each brand from each store in even one product category is a lot of data. Many tests require that related product categories be studied, too.

The richness of the data may make fewer stores necessary for market tests than in the past, but it's still a lot of data. Even when records from all stores are combined, weekly printouts provide almost nine times as much data as we've been accustomed to getting from Nielsen's bimonthly reports. Systems for data reduction clearly are needed.

Scanners *are* going to revolutionize information gathering in grocery store marketing. But if you're working on a new product today, don't wait for them.

... But Outlook Is Changing

BY MARY BYRNES

NEW YORK—The checkout scanner, a promise that failed to pan out right away, may finally be approaching its potential. Hampered early on by astronomical hardware costs, Universal Product Code problems and the overabundance of unwieldy data they generated, scanners have had trouble winning acceptance among test marketers. A number of prevailing factors now appear to be changing the outlook.

■ Though still expensive, the hardware is now more affordable, thanks to the resistance of electronic data processing prices to inflation and the entry of new competitors into the marketplace. Chain store owners—increasingly more savvy about edp—are also discovering that the cost of scanners can be offset by more efficient store operation. That means more scanners are in use, which makes sampling easier for the test marketer.

There are even more significant developments on the software side. Here, leading scanner services, such as A. C. Nielsen Co., Northbrook, Ill., and Selling Areas-Marketing Inc., New York, are developing computer programs to transform the usual deluge of scanner data into comprehensible, accessible report form.

Blips are replacing rings at checkout counters nationwide.

■ "Scanning is really still in its infancy," says Ted Karonias, vp-scanning service market research at Nielsen. "But we've learned a lot from our early problems. Scanning provides masses of data that were never available before and that just can't be had any other way. We've overcome many of the difficulties that involved an excess of data, but there are still a lot of numbers. In the very near future, however, we'll be able to manipulate those numbers even more effectively than we do now to produce even more refined reports.

"Faster data means faster decisions on the part of marketing strategists. That means we who produce that data have to be cautious about how we compile and present it."

At Nielsen, he explains, that means quality control and an ongoing effort to present clients with a "total picture" of a scanning period.

"Our reports," he says, "indicate not just what's scanned, but what's not. Not just what's captured in the data, but what's not. Plus causal data that's beyond the computer that we get from field reps—weather conditions, what the competition did, local ads and promotions, news—anything in the environment that affects supermarket sales."

■ At SAMI, the scanner pioneer, project manager Frank Smith reports a similar effort to refine data and deliver a full market picture. "We're experts at dealing with masses of data," he maintains. "We know how to array it and apply it." SAMI, like Nielsen, has developed a software system that generates comprehensive yet comprehendable reports.

"We're virtually the leaders in reporting warehouse withdrawal data," says Mr. Smith, pointing to SAMI's electronic method of matching UPC code to its own codes to refine data.

One development of interest to test marketers is the growth of electronic diary panels to supplement basic scanner data. SAMI, which was first with the system, selects participants from a market, equips each with a special coded plastic purchasing card and prepares reports on their demographics and shopping habits. As an incentive, each participant receives a discount at the supermarket equaling approximately 2% of his total monthly purchases.

Now in operation in six stores, SAMI's electronic diary panel can provide quick, highly detailed buyer profiles, including everything from response to couponing to effects of in-store promotions to the impact of a tv campaign. It reveals which products are most likely to be bought together and the impact of one purchase upon another.

■ "One of the most important things the diary can do for a client," says Mr. Smith, "is brand franchise share requirement analysis. This shows a client what his major competition is, what brands the buyers are selecting when they don't buy his. Often, clients discover that what they had singled out as their competition isn't their real competition at all. And that brings about a shift to a more effective marketing strategy."

Nielsen's electronic diary panel is still in its first stages, operating in two Rochester, N.Y., stores. Like SAMI's, it is designed to reflect buyer profiles and the impact of various marketing activities.

"Our diary is really in its presentation stage now," says Mr. Karonias. "We have a strong belief in its commercial value and in its inevitable success. But it is expensive, as is any diary method of this nature and magnitude, and we're now attempting to convince our clients that it is worth a considerable investment."

A third company, Market Science Associates, Des Plaines, Ill., has developed MARKETRAX, a large scale UPC scanner panel system. The system, which was put into operation in October, consists of about 2,500 households in Greater Los Angeles whose grocery purchases are tracked at the time of purchase in the stores they shop in. Among the options the system allows are tests of alternative pricing, measurements of coupon effectiveness and judgments of packaging.

■ Even with these developments, however, both Nielsen and SAMI still find capturing and transmitting scanner data can be the source of some problems. Although more and more products—even meat and produce items—bear the distinctive zebra labels, many items remain uncoded. Many of those that *are* labeled are done so inefficiently. A poor printing job, too light a color of ink on the label or too dark a background may cause a package to escape the scanner's "eye."

There are still difficulties, too, in getting data from the stores to edp centers. Scanner data, now recorded on disc or cassette, are often delayed in shipment to the main computer. And delays can blunt the value of sales figures.

Still, it looks as though the success of scanners is inevitable, if somewhat delayed in coming. "One of the biggest boosts we're getting," says Mr. Karonias, "is in the increasing acceptance of scanners. We projected [in 1979] that the number would reach 1,425 by the year's end. And by the end of '80, that should double. There are about 100 being added every month.

■ "The more scanners in use, the more pressure there will be for manufacturers to solve the labeling problem. That will make our work easier. And the more scanners there are, the closer we will come to being able to build a national sample."

Even if it was "no sale" for scanners yesterday, Mr. Karonias believes, as does Mr. Smith, that the story will be different tomorrow: Scanners are not just here to stay but will become an essential tool in market research.

Targeting Product Ideas

BY ROBERT H. HOMAN

NEW YORK—Market segmentation, the concept that fueled the consumer marketing revolution of the '60s and '70s, may be running out of steam as we approach the '80s.

Marketers, it appears, will have to search for other methods of attracting consumers to new products. Targeting a product to a specific audience is losing effectiveness, especially as the potential number of audiences dwindles.

But that's not to say that market segmentation has not served a valuable purpose. Indeed, it played a vital part in the evolution of consumer marketing as we know it today.

Consumer marketing itself got off the ground in the years just after World War II. The category penetration of deodorants, for example, was virtually nil before the war, especially among males. But every GI got a deodorant in his hygiene kit from Uncle Sam, and when he returned home, he began to use his wife's or buy his own.

■ Product differentiation grew, but only by form—cream, spray, stick, roll-on and finally aerosol— or by ingredients, from deodorant to antiperspirant. The market became saturated with me-too brands.

Robert H. Homan is President of New Products Resources in New York.

Then came market segmentation. Manufacturers began to look for problems existing brands weren't solving. In the late '60s, for instance, Gillette found that aerosol propellants stung and burned women after they shaved their underarms. Result: Soft 'N Dri, a nonsting formula positioned for women.

Revlon found another niche, the problem perspirer. In the early '70s, the company repositioned its high-priced Mitchum Antiperspirant for the segment that felt regular brands didn't work, but evidently Mitchum did.

Today the market is saturated once again, but this time with differentiated products. The problem is that, as in a lot of other markets, most consumer needs have been filled. Those that haven't can't be met technically and aren't worth the effort or they may have been identified by the competitor, who perhaps will be able to do a better job faster.

■ Take the antiperspirant market again. An analysis would reveal that the most annoying, most frequent problem not being solved satisfactorily by current brands is "wetness." Take care of that problem and there's an excellent chance of becoming the instant category leader. Gillette's Dry One is taking a shot at it.

Even if a manufacturing company is smart enough to come up with a product need that it can do something about, there may be other smart people with the same information working on the same

55

problem. That may be the reason we often see three or four companies introduce virtually the same product at the same time in the same market.

The question then arises: Where are new product opportunities to be found?

I believe the search must expand beyond the specific category that is the subject of a new product exploration. To identify clues to successful new concepts in the subject category, one must scan a random selection of related, as well as unrelated, product categories.

To accomplish this, New Products Resources has designed a new search technique we call S.C.A.A.N. (Satellite Category Attribute Analysis). A few illustrations from some of our recent projects will show how the process works.

■ The example involves working with totally unrelated categories.

A major chemical company was interested in building a franchise in the rapidly growing do-it-yourself segment of the $29 billion auto care market. Part of this effort was to come from internal product development, applying the company's high technology capability to some important problem areas.

To find clues to innovative ways to relate this technology to the auto care market, we looked at a variety of other product categories. Most of them involved things in which we had direct experience or available information. We looked not at market sizes, growth trends and other hard data, but at potentially relevant consumer behavior and product applications.

The results were presented according to the auto care "task" (or problem to be solved) and the satellite category providing the concept clue. In each case, we asked ourselves a question that related behavior in the satellite category to the task or problem in the subject category. Then with advice from the company's technical staff, we

were able to come up with some innovative solutions.

For example:

• **Task:** Changing the oil.

Satellite category: Baby care. What's the relationship between changing a baby's diaper and changing a car's oil?

Both involved the collection and disposal of waste. The disposable diaper acts as a one way valve. It is totally absorbent on the inside, yet completely sealed on the outside. Mom simply removes the diaper from baby and throws it away.

The problems with changing oil involve both collection and disposal. First, you put a container under the car, open the crankcase and let the oil drain into a container and not on the garage floor. Now that you've collected the dirty oil, what do you do with it? The garbage collector won't take it. You can't pour it down the sink. You're stuck with it.

Solution: A large floor mat, constructed from the same material as a disposable diaper is placed under the car. Open the crankcase, let the oil pour out, then roll up the mat and dispose it in the garbage. (Technology and excess manufacturing capacity were available in the company, since it had aborted the rollout of its baby diaper product.)

• **Task:** Touching up nicks in the car's finish.

Satellite category: Health care. What does plastic surgery have to do with touching up nicks?

You decide to touch up those nicks and scratches your car has been collecting in the shopping center parking lot. So you get a can of Evening Blue paint to match your Evening Blue sedan. But you find the colors don't match. Why? Oxidation and exposure to the sun have changed the color of your car. Evening has faded to Afternoon Blue.

We looked at how a plastic surgeon handles burns. He grafts good skin from another part of the body to the damaged surface. We asked the research & development staff whether it could chemically transfer paint from another part of the car to the damaged surfce.

Solution: A small pad can remove a small quantity of paint from areas not visible such as the lip of the hood and the rocker panels, and transfer it to the scratch area for a perfect match.

• **Task:** Repairing dents.

Satellite category: Food preparation. What does baking a cake have to do with repairing a dent?

The standard method of repairing a dent at the local body shop is to bang it out. But for the do-it-yourself mechanic, it may require tools he doesn't have and a skill that, if lacking, may turn a dent into a bump.

Solution: We found that a simple, foolproof way to repair dents is to tackle the job the way you'd bake a cake.

To bake a cake you first fill a cake pan with a liquid batter. When you bake it, the heat from the oven turns the liquid into a solid cake. Working with the technical group, we conceived an aerosol that dispenses a creamy liquid. Just fill the dent with the material. It slowly hardens as it adheres to the sides of the cavity. Then just sand it down and paint it over. No more dent.

■ The auto care market provides examples of creating unique solutions to identifiable problems within a product category by searching for clues in seemingly unrelated categories.

Another example of how the process works involves stretching the mind slightly beyond current business to related kinds of products.

A major food processor asked us to explore the multi-billion-dollar sandwich filling business. We found the space between two slices of bread a pretty boring place. Outside hot dogs and hamburgers, each day nearly nine in ten sandwiches were being filled with either bologna, ham, cheese, tuna salad, peanut butter or jelly.

With variety available in other food types, it wasn't necessary to go any further for some interesting sandwich concept clues.

We saw an opportunity to translate popular main meal entrees into exciting, convenient sandwich fillings that can be served hot or cold:

• Shish kebob sandwich slices with marinated charcoal-grilled flavor meat and slices of green and red peppers, onions and tomatoes.

• Barbecue sandwich slices with crisp, glazed and barbecue-flavored beef, pork, chicken and ham.

• Southern fried sandwich slices with breaded and fried chicken, pork and ham.

We looked at making existing sandwich fillings more appealing to children by using the unique shapes, forms, colors and flavor combinations found in children's cookies and crackers.

We looked at desserts. The jelly roll cake gave us a clue to combine popular food types usually eaten as part of the same meal, but unavailable as a sandwich filling— turkey and chestnut stuffing or ham and pineapple dressing, for example.

■ Auto care and sandwich fillings represent markets in which this creative search technique involves itself with creating unique solutions to identifiable problems. But how do you create unique concepts in markets in which a number of readily identifiable problems do not exist.

Take the candy bar market. Even with growing concern about cavities and empty calories, it continues to be a billion dollar business. But historically, successful new products have been hard to come by, and old brands are nearly impossible to kill. What market today has so many money-making brands that were around when your grandfather was a boy? (Hershey's, Nestle's, Oh Henry, Fifth Avenue, Butterfinger and even a brand named after President Grover Cleveland's daughter, Baby Ruth.)

An examination of the candy bar market indicated that perhaps the underlying reason for the lack of success of new brands was that none of them was really new. We analyzed the ingredients, flavors and textures of 56 brands and found very limited differences. All were chocolate flavored. Most contained something crunchy— generally nuts—and something chewy such as caramel, nougat or marshmallow. None was differentiated by positioning.

To look for clues to new concepts it was apparent we had to look beyond the candy bar market.

First, we examined some regulated confectionery categories. We observed that hard candies come in fruit flavors, not chocolate. Why not a fruit-flavored candy bar?

Then we asked ourselves some fundamental questions that evidently had not been asked by the industry experts:

What is a candy bar? A form of sweet.

What are some other popular sweets? Ice cream, cake, pie, pudding, gelatin, yogurt, cookies, fruit.

How are these other sweets eaten? As a snack, but also as a dessert.

These answers provided clues to an entirely new candy bar concept: A candy bar with a wafer center as light as pastry, coated with a strawberry-flavored frosting and topped with a creamy swirl. The product was positioned as a unique alternative to run-of-the-mill chocolate bars, providing favorite dessert flavors in portable candy bar form.

Repeat Purchases Are Key

BY JACK J. HONOMICHL

NEW YORK—Of all questions asked in new product research, this is the one deemed crucial by many people: "Is my product getting the repeat purchasing necessary to ensure success?"

A definitive answer depends on normative data—a base of case histories where known repeat rates can be related to the ultimate success of products in the real world marketplace.

A valuable contribution toward that end has been provided by NPD Research Inc., the largest U.S. panel company. Over the years NPD has compiled case histories of 120 new products in which repeat purchases were measured via continuous, diary-type panels in either test market(s) or regional or national rollouts.

After each survey, NPD asked client companies to evaluate the ultimate success of the products. Thirty-six were considered "successful," 36 were labeled "marginal" and the remaining 48 were deemed "failures."

■ The results of this analysis can be seen in Table 1. Note that in the 36 "successful" cases, the mean true repeat rate was 64%—or, of all households that bought the new product, more than six out of ten made at least one repeat purchase within a year. The mode in this group was 55%. The range was from a high of 80% or more repeat purchases to a low of 45%.

■ Included in this analysis was a range of consumer goods—human and pet foods, beverages, paper and health and beauty aid products, some of which have a long purchase cycle; a wait of six or more months is required to see if an original purchaser eventually "repeats." In a fast-turn product class, of course, that can be seen in a relatively short time.

Back to Table 1. With those products considered "marginally successful," the mean repeat rate was 47%, and the mode was 45%. The range was from a high of 65% to a low of 25%.

A high repeat rate alone—and 60% to 65% is high—is not enough to spell success; it can be a high repeat from what was a dangerously low trial base in the first place. Or the repeat purchases can be stimulated by extraordinarily attractive deal inducements; when trial users have to face up to full shelf price, too many drop out.

Finally, with those case histories in which the product was considered a "failure," the mean repeat rate was 39%, and the mode was 35%. The range was from a high of 55% to a low of 25% or less.

■ To people who like simplistic rules of thumb, these data say that a repeat rate of 64% or more probably means success; a rate of 47% means "maybe" and a rate of 39% usually means "failure."

But, as with any normative data, such conclusions can be misleading. Let's take a closer look at the NPD data. In Table 2, these same

120 case histories are broken into five groups—human foods, pet foods, beverages, paper products and h&ba—and trial and repeat norms are shown along a time continuum. Measurements for pet foods are based on animal households only; others are based on all households in the market.

With new human food products, for instance, the norm is when 9% of the households makes one trial purchase within the first four months the product is on the market. This has grown to 13% by the sixth month, 15% by the ninth month and 19% by the 12th month. The number of case histories here,

---

Table 1

IMPORTANCE OF REPEAT-TRUE REPEAT RATES FOR 120 NEW PRODUCTS

Distribution of cases where repeat was at least:	Per cent of products classified as:		
	"Successful" 30%	"Marginal" 30%	"Failures" 40%
80%, or more	4%	—	—
75	14	—	—
70	14	—	—
65	14	4%	—
60	7	7	—
55	29	11	3%
50	14	7	11
45	4	32	16
40	—	14	13
35	—	11	21
30	—	7	13
25	—	7	21
Less than 25	—	—	3
Mean true repeat rate	64%	47%	39%

Source: NPD Research New Product Normative Data Base

Table 2

SUMMARY OF NEW PRODUCT NORMS

Cumulative Brand Trial

Product Class	4 Months After Introduction	6 Months	9 Months	12 Months	Number of Case Histories
Human Food	9%	13%	16%	19%	28-65
Pet Food	14	20	25	29	9
Beverage	10	12	14	17	8-13
Paper	6	9	11	14	12-20
Health & Beauty Aids	5	7	10	12	16-24

Cumulative Per Cent of Triers Repeating

Human Food	26%	33%	37%	41%	27-63
Pet Food	42	54	58	60	9
Beverage	35	43	45	47	8-13
Paper	26	31	36	30	12-20
Health & Beauty Aids	20	27	33	36	16-24

Source: NPD RESEARCH Normative Data Base

28 to 65, indicates that although 65 case histories are represented, not all were measured for the full 12 months; only 28 went that far.

Looking down to Cumulative Per Cent of Triers Repeating in Table 2, we see that for human food products, the normative repeat rate at month four was 26%—that is, of all households that had tried the product to date, 26% had made at least one repeat purchase. This penetration topped off at 41% after 12 months.

■ Obviously, the trial rate that can be expected varies significantly from one type of product to another, as do the repeat levels.

Because trial is the name of the game in new product introductions, various devices are tested at the test market stage, and one case history provided by NPD Research shows very dramatically what product sampling programs can do to hype purchasing.

With this new product, which was tested in a commonly used test market area over a 14-month period, there were two sampling programs tested. In one of them (a), households were sent a full-size package of the product, a two to three-month supply. In the other (b) households were sent a one-time use trial pouch of the product, plus a coupon toward purchase. A third group (c), the control, received nothing. Of this control group, (c), 14% purchased the product eventually, at the 14 months point.

Both test groups, (a) and (b), eventually had 24% trial, but the development pattern was much different: Group (b) took off at a fast rate; group (a) was relatively sluggish, which is to be expected since trial users received a two to three-month supply of the product, and that postponed the need to purchase. But the end result was basically the same, and the cost of sampling could be evaluated against the end result of not sampling.

Obviously, while such case histories and normative data are interesting by themselves, they still represent just part of the story. There are many more variables—advertising weight, copy, distribution, product quality (good trial kills a bad product fast) and competitive reactions to new product testing. Still, the more codified the experience in the public domain, the better.

Test Promotions, Too

BY ANDREW TARSHIS

FLORAL PARK, N.Y.—What test marketing has been for new products, it is becoming as much for consumer promotions.

The questions marketers are asking with respect to their promotions are similar to those asked when test marketing new products. How many buyers will I attract? Am I attracting buyers of competitive brands or wasting my promotion by simply attracting my current buyers? Will all buyers be induced to repurchase, or am I simply attracting deal-oriented buyers who are likely to switch away on their next purchase occasion? What types of promotion vehicles work best to achieve marketing goals? Coupons? Free samples? High value? Low value?

The need for answers to those questions is becoming ever more critical.

■ One overwhelming reason is that the growth in coupons over the last few years has reached incredible proportions. In 1978, according to A. C. Nielsen Co., 73 billion manufacturer coupons were delivered, representing a 100% increase over just three years ago.

From 1970 through 1975, the rate of coupon growth was slow and steady, but then in 1976 the rate took off. And there has been little letup. Preliminary counts indicate

that about 85 billion coupons were delivered in 1979.

Another reason for the interest in coupons is that manufacturers are shifting their budgets from trade to consumer promotions. In 1977, according to a Donnelly Survey only 33% of total promotion dollars went to consumer promotions; by 1979 it had increased to 42%. Studies have shown, meanwhile, that as much as two-thirds of the money offered the trade for promotions has not been used.

A third reason is that cents-off couponing has become the most important promotion tool for major manufacturers, according to the Donnelley survey. In 1976, fewer than half of the companies responding to the survey ranked coupons as their most important promotion tool whereas in 1979 almost three-fourths of them did.

■ Much of this increasing need for a better understanding of consumer promotions has resulted in marketers' looking for ways to test market promotions. One of the most successful approaches has been the use of established test market purchase diary panels.

NPD Research has 35,000 families participating in ongoing diary panels in more than 50 different test markets throughout the U.S. These panels range in size from several hundred to several thousand families.

The NPD panels consist of families who record their purchases of package goods as the purchases are made.

For each purchase made, panel-

Andrew Tarshis is a senior vp of NPD Research, Floral Park, NY.

ists record the date of purchase, brand name, number of units bought, price paid, whether it involved a special deal, the type and name of the store and substantial information to identify product attributes. The critical element is that a high degree of detail on each promotion—e.g., 7¢ store coupon, 25¢ magazine coupon, 10¢ store special—is recorded by the panel member.

■ The advantages of diary data are clear. They involve no recall, complete item descriptions and records of purchases from all outlets, not just scanner equipped stores.

This last point should not be overlooked. Studies have shown that families who shop in more than one store are more deal-oriented than families who shop in only one store. Consequently, promotion tests done only in scanner equipped stores tend to understate the full impact of promotions.

Diary panels, furthermore, are used extensively to evaluate new products in test market, and many of the same analytical measures (trial, repeat, brand switching) are not only applicable, but very important, to the successful test marketing of promotions.

How would a promotion test market be established?

Assume we wanted to test different coupon values. Panel members in three markets—e.g., Albany, Charlotte and Tucson—would be selected and divided into balanced subsets. In one case, for example, one-third would recive a 10¢ coupon, one-third a 25¢ coupon and one-third would act as a control group and receive no special promotion.

■ This design eliminates the typical bias of using one market as a test market and another as a control, or one group of stores as test stores and another group as a control.

Also, each cell is demographically balanced to ensure that there

are no biases. And because total flexibility exists in choosing markets, it is assured the tester will get an adequate geographic dispersion.

Over the past year, NPD Research has carried out numerous promotion tests for clients as part of new product test market analyses. Some tests involved coupons, some free samples, and some involved both. Results were as follows:

• Both coupons and free samples tended to boost trial or first purchasing.

• Free samples were especially effective in generating first purchase for superior products, but they were less effective for "me-too" types.

• Coupons induced quicker trial puchasing than free samples, but repeat purchases tended to be greater through samples.

• Coupons tended to be more effective in the short run, but over time the balance tipped in favor of free samples.

A closer look at the impact of coupons on trials or first purchases shows that, for the new brands involved in a case we studied, an average of 7.4% of households made a purchase in the first six months if they were not subjected to any special promotion. By contrast, among the households who received a coupon, 15.1% purchased the brand. The coupons, in other words, resulted in twice the trial level as would have occurred without a promotion.

■ A similar result was seen for the free samples. Compared with a first purchase rate of 11.4% among households not receiving any promotion, 16% of those that received the free sample purchased the brand.

Comparing the relative effects of coupons and free samples shows that coupons boosted trials on first purchases by more than 100% whereas free samples, on average, led to a 40% increase.

One interesting thing about these differences is that the effect of coupons tended to be fairly consistent for all cases—varying from a low of +70% to a high of +140%—while the impact of free samples was quite varied and, in fact, related to the quality of the product being tested. All of this was evident in looking at the relative trial rates for three new products, one of which ultimately was a tremendous success, one a "me-too" product that was marginally successful and one ultimately deemed a failure.

■ For the successful new product, the free sample just about doubled trial purchasing, compared with the effect coupons had. Compared with a first purchase rate of 13% for families who *did not* receive the free sample, 25% of the families who *did* receive the sample went on to purchase the brand.

For the product that was not unique, but which eventually carved out an acceptable, but not superb, market share, the percentage of families who went on to purchase after receiving the free sample was the same as the percentage who purchased without the inducement of a sample.

On the bottom are the results for a brand that has little appeal. Interestingly, fewer families who received the sample went on to purchase the brand than families not receiving the sample. If nothing else, this indicates that promotion test marketing may serve as an early warning system for products that may be doomed to failure due to intrinsic weaknesses.

Although important, these rates of first purchase are only one side of the coin; the other side, of course, is repeat purchasing, which in this particular case provides some enlightening differences.

■ When families made their first purchase with a coupon, they were less likely to repurchase than families whose first purchase was made without a coupon.

So one basic conclusion we have is that coupons tend to attract more buyers, as was seen before, but, as we see here, these buyers had a lower probability of repurchasing.

For free samples, in contrast to coupons, the repurchase rate tended to be higher. Over-all, 35.7% of the families who purchased after receiving a sample went on to repurchase, compared with only 31.8% of the control group. This positive impact was consistent across all brands, in contrast to the first purchase effect, in which product quality played a role.

These results so far have been based on six months of data. When 12 months of purchasing are analyzed, we see some interesting developments. In the six-month period, for example, coupons tended to produce more first purchasing than samples did.

After 12 months, however, the difference actually narrowed. After six months, coupons resulted in a trial purchase rate of 18%, compared with 11% for the free sample. After 12 months, this 7% difference narrowed to a 4% point difference.

■ One obvious reason is that a sample takes some time to use up, whereas a coupon tends to be redeemed much more quickly.

Putting all these findings together for both trial and repeat purchasing indicates that, in the short run, coupons tend to outperform samples, but in the long run, samples tend to provide better results.

In the six month period, the coupon effect on first purchasing (18% vs. 11%) outweighed the free sample effect on repeat (29% vs. 21%) so that in total the coupon led to more repeaters over-all, 38 per 1,000 vs. 32 per 1,000.

After 12 months, however, as the difference in first purchase narrowed, the over-all impact in terms of repeaters per 1,000 tipped in favor of free samples, resulting in 10% more repeaters than the coupons.

This differential can even be considered conservative, because only first repeat purchases were examined here. Over time, as repeat becomes more important and depth of repeat becomes a factor, the free sample would result in even a stronger performance.

There are several factors that need to be evaluated before one adopts a free sample strategy instead of a coupon one. The first is cost. Samples are more expensive than coupons and the additional business generated may not offset these costs.

Also, because coupons lead to quicker trial purchasing may mean that a coupon plan integrated with some follow-up promotion—bounce-back coupon, in-store promotion—may result in better performance than a sample or equal performance at a lower cost.

And do not forget the factor of product quality. If a brand does not test well against competition, it doesn't make any sense to have a costly sampling campaign; it makes more sense to go with a coupon campaign, thereby reducing both costs and sales objectives.

■ In summary, what has been shown here only scratches the surface of promotion test marketing. The results presented relate only tests of the effect of coupons and free samples on trial and repeat for new products. A similar approach works for existing brands and for other types of promotions.

Just as in test marketing new products, the aim of test marketing promotions is to achieve a better understanding of how various promotions influence consumer purchasing behavior. This way, marketers can make better decisions on how to allocate their ever-increasing promotion budgets.

End of the Testing Era

BY GEOFFREY E. MEREDITH

SAN FRANCISCO—We are at the end of an era of test marketing. Within the next several years, conventional test marketing of new package goods should become almost totally dead as an effective marketing tool.

There are two reasons:

• More and more frequently, a new product test entry generates a defensive response by competition, and these unusual or unexpected responses can and usually do destroy test projectability. The possibility of purposely disrupting a test has always existed, but until the 1970s such defensive efforts by competitors were comparatively rare. When they occurred, they were often either too feeble or too late to impede a valid "read."

Today, however, an immediate and violent test market defensive response to a product test by a "major" package goods manufacturer is so common that the opportunity to project test market results confidently has become rare.

• There is increasing evidence that competitors today are able and willing to react much more quickly to new test market introductions—reacting not just disruptively, but in fact imitating and preempting the test brand. This happens because instances of a new entry based on a proprietary

Geoffrey E. Meredith is senior vp-management supervisor at Botsford Ketchum, San Francisco.

or difficult-to-duplicate technology are uncommon today.

New products, moreover, often appear in test at the same time a competitor is developing similar products. In such situations, the competitor can accelerate development of its similar product, evaluate it in other ways and expand broadscale *without* test marketing, thus preempting the original brand.

The motive for preemption can be either defensive, as in the case of a competitor trying to protect an existing brand from being hurt by a new entry, or opportunistic, as in the case of a new marketer in the category trying to become established first. In either case, rather than aiding the new product development process, even a "successful" market test often can cause an expensive failure of a national entry.

Today, the quickness and effectiveness of competitive responses to test markets demand a fundamental rethinking of how to launch new products. If test marketing is as likely to *cause* a marketing disaster as it is to *prevent* one, other techniques will have to be used.

Two Case Histories

The defensive preemption can be illustrated by what happened when Batter 'n Bake met Crisp 'n Tender. For at least 10 years, one of General Foods' major brands has been Shake 'n Bake dry chicken coating mix. Shake 'n Bake has historically held more than a 90% share of the $60,000,000-plus

In 1973, General Foods' Batter 'n Bake ...

... took on Betty Crocker's Crisp 'n Tender.

chicken coating category and, as its nickname, "profit in a pouch," implies, it probably returns considerably more than $10,000,000 a year in pretax profits to General Foods, despite substantial market outlays (advertising spending was more than $13,000,000 in 1977, for example).

As a result, when General Mills began a test market of Crisp 'n Tender liquid batter chicken coating mix in February, 1973, General Foods was more than mildly interested. General Foods watched Crisp 'n Tender's test market progress closely; the product appeared to be at least marginally successful.

Accordingly, in August, 1973, General Foods launched a similar liquid batter coating called Batter 'n Bake. Presumably, GF's thinking was that if liquid chicken coating mixes were a viable competitor

to Shake 'n Bake, we want our own entry and that the category, perhaps, could support one entry but not two, in which case the problem would go away.

In any case, Batter 'n Bake was introduced nationally, without test marketing, and received nearly $10,000,000 in advertising and promotion support over the next two years. Nearly all of this represented a net decrease in profit to General Foods, since neither Batter 'n Bake nor Crisp 'n Tender established much of a consumer franchise. General Mills, however, withdrew Crisp 'n Tender from the marketplace, and shortly thereafter, General Foods pulled its support from Batter 'n Bake; it too soon faded away.

This was a classic case of defensive preemption via competitive test market monitoring.

The case of opportunistic preemption can be exemplified by the case of Mazola No-Stick *vs.* Cooking Ease.

In 1973, the Clorox Co. began testing a new entry in the aerosol nonstick cooking spray category, which at that time was dominated by American Home Products' Pam. The Clorox entry, Cooking Ease, appeared by early spring of 1974 to be highly successful in test market, despite increased marketing efforts by Pam.

As plans for national expansion were being prepared, however, a new competitor appeared: Mazola No-Stick, marketed by CPC International. Mazola No-Stick was introduced broadly into about a third of the U.S., without test marketing, and quickly expanded broadscale before Cooking Ease.

No-Stick rapidly became the second major brand in the market behind Pam. It remains the No. 2 brand today, while Cooking Ease is no longer a major factor in the marketplace.

Subsequent statements by CPC spokesmen indicated clearly that the key factor in the expansion decision was Cooking Ease: If the Cooking Ease test market had not been so successful, Mazola No-Stick would have been introduced far more cautiously—a clear case of a test market success causing a national failure.

The Ideal

Thus far we have seen how conventional test marketing has contributed to the downfall of selected new package goods entries. This in turn raises the question, "What should a testing methodology do?"

Although cost is obviously a factor, it is clear that the two single most important features that a testing methodology should possess is the ability to predict correctly the success or failure of a more broadscale effort, while maintaining confidentiality. A "cheap" test that predicts "failure" or "success" inaccurately is no bargain. And a nonconfidential test obviously can be self-defeating.

Predictability and confidentiality, moreover, are a function of the following five elements, all of which influence predictability and which compose the functions of an "ideal" testing methodology:

• To predict sales volume accurately, through a correct estimation of consumer response to the product and product promise in terms of trial rate, repurchase rate and purchase cycle length.

• To be quick, so that changes in the marketing environment do not invalidate national predictability.

• To be unsusceptible to unusual competitive reactions—again, an odd competitive reaction in a testing situation tends to mar national predictability.

• To be inaccessable to competition, ideally in all regards—product and advertising—but in terms of consumer response, at the minimum.

• To accurately predict trade response, so as to gauge distribution levels.

These five are the most important factors a testing methodology should have, because they affect over-all predictability, and they measure uncontrollable variables—the consumer, the competition, the trade and the environment. There are two controllable areas, however, where the testing methodology can be valuable: It can help "fine tune" the marketing plan, and it can help the buying and manufacturing departments by providing empirical data for more precise cost and profit estimates and by providing practice runs so that manufacturing problems can be ironed out.

Given the above criteria for an "ideal" testing methodology, the following section examines the three basic types of testing approach: Full scale market testing, controlled minimarket testing and laboratory testing.

Testing Alternatives

Full-scale market testing, according to our model, falls short on six of the seven key attributes an ideal

Cases that make the point

Listed below are a few recent examples of opportunistic preemption that come readily to mind; in each instance, a brand that was apparently successful in test market was copied and preempted nationally by a competitor who did not test market:

Brand in test market	Preemptor
Arm in Arm Deodorant (Helene Curtis)	Arm & Hammer Deodorant (Church & Dwight)
Maxim (General Foods)	Taster's Choice (Nestle)
High Yield Coffee (Hills Bros.)	Folger's Flakes (Procter & Gamble)
Prima Salsa Tomato Sauce (Hunt-Wesson)	Ragu Extra Thick & Zesty Chesebrough-Pond's

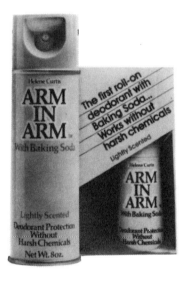

testing methodology should provide. It does give a good measure of trade responsiveness, and in fact is the only way to determine it. Full-scale test marketing, however, is slow, open to competitive responses (either disruptive or pre-emptive), cumbersome as a tool to evaluate different marketing mixes and costly. Most importantly, it is proving to be not very predictive of national results.

Minimarket testing fares somewhat better. Because outside suppliers are used to force distribution, there is no lengthy sell-in period, and testing time is, consequently, shortened. Because of this—and because minimarkets are not routinely monitored by Nielsen, SAMI, etc.—competition has somewhat less time to react, and less information to act on. And because the markets themselves are smaller, marketing costs are substantially reduced. Also because of the smaller markets used, however, even unimpeded results are less reliable than those of full-scale test marketing.

"Laboratory" test markets emerge as the best alternative. There are a number of independent marketing companies that, as suppliers, offer this kind of test marketing system. In addition, many manufacturers or advertising agencies have developed their own customized approaches. All use basically the same technique: The target customers are exposed to test commercials and competitive product commercials in a simulated television show environment. They then may purchase the test product or competitive product in a simulated (in some cases actual) store. Those who purchase the product use it in the home. Telephone research follows in order to elicit reactions to the product, usage information and repurchase intent. Share figures are then computed by applying "corrective" factors derived from previous testing norms.

Based on extensive experience, the "laboratory" test approach has the following advantages over conventional test marketing:

• It can predict on par with a full-scale test market approach—and with reasonable accuracy.

• It is fast. In most instances, a laboratory test market can conduct a full market evaluation in 12 to 14 weeks. This is months, or even years, quicker than conventional test marketing methods.

• It is confidential. Competitors do not have the opportunity to pre-empt test brands, or disrupt test markets artificially.

• Various marketing mixes can be easily and cheaply tested. It should be noted, however, that sales and share estimates based on, for example, differing levels of advertising support are probably not terribly precise.

This approach, of course, has its disadvantages, too.

• It does not provide any measure of trade response, because distribution is forced.

• It does not help buying or manufacturing "practice" for national expansion, because required product quantities are so small.

• It is probably not as precise as an unimpeded test market in terms of predictability. The key words in this statement are "precise" and "unimpeded": I believe that a large test market that is not "muddied" by unusual competitive activity (or rendered invalid by changes in the competitive environment over-all) is probably a more precise prediction of market share than laboratory testing. Laboratory testing tends to supply directional estimates, ones that say "success" or "failure" but cannot absolutely quantify the *levels* of each. To the extent that an extremely precise estimate of share is vital, laboratory testing may be at a disadvantage.

• It does not provide broadbased consumer feedback over time on actual product performance, as would be the case in the marketplace. However, extended large-scale in-home testing conducted with the start of a laboratory test market can pinpoint any major consumer reservations.

Market Experience

How does all of this translate into actual experience?

Our experience has shown that conventional test marketing has not been a very accurate predictor of the national share, except in the case of the earliest example measured.

In all cases, the laboratory procedure was a far more accurate predictor of test market share than the test market was of national share. The reason for this is that during the lengthy test market period, competition was able to react either defensively or preemptively so as to make the later expansion unsuccessful.

If the brands we studied had been launched nationally without a revealing and time-consuming test market, I believe the laboratory test market share predictions would have been validated broadscale. Four cases were incidents in which a competitor was able to read the brand's test markets and launch a preemptive copy broadscale before the brand could be expanded. A fifth was an aerosol product that was expanded just at the time the "ozone depletion" controversy appeared, and this

(coupled with a general economic downturn) spelled failure. Finally, a sixth brand never expanded, based on disappointing laboratory and test market results.

Far from helping a marketer to establish a successful new product, our experience has been that in today's rapidly changing world, a test market often insures failure.

What Can Be Done?

It is clear from our experiences that laboratory testing is much faster, more confidential and less expensive than traditional testing. Because it is faster and confidential, it is also a better predictor. Thus, the inescapable conclusion is that new products should be launched broadscale *without* conventional test marketing when: A laboratory test market indicates a clear-cut success, when extended in-home panel tests indicate no major product reservations and when the time available before competition can expropriate the new product's attributes is short.

From now on, in most cases marketers are going to have to bite the bullet. They will have to accept the admittedly somewhat less precise, "success/failure" predictions of laboratory test marketing as the basis for new product national introduction decisions.

Attributes of Testing Alternatives

Attribute	Full-scale test market	Minimarket test	Laboratory test market
Predictor of volume and share	Poor	Fair	Good
Timing	Very slow, 9-12 mos. minimum	Slow, 2-3 mos. faster than full-scale test	Very fast, 12-14 weeks
Can be influenced by competition (i.e., heavyups, etc.)	Yes	Yes	No
Confidentiality	Completely open to competition	Not confidential, but not monitored by Nielsen, etc.	Confidential
Can predict trade response	Yes	No	No
Can test alternative marketing mixes easily and cheaply	No	Yes, but to a lesser extent than laboratory test marketing	Yes, although accuracy is not precise
Cost	High-over $500M	Medium—about $175M	Low—about $60M